# Coalfields regeneration

**Dealing with the consequences of industrial decline**

Katy Bennett, Huw Beynon and Ray Hudson

The POLICY

P ~ P

PRESS

First published in Great Britain in March 2000 by

The Policy Press
34 Tyndall's Park Road
Bristol BS8 1PY
UK

Tel no   +44 (0)117 954 6800
Fax no   +44 (0)117 973 7308
E-mail   tpp@bristol.ac.uk
http://www.bristol.ac.uk/Publications/TPP

© The Policy Press and the Joseph Rowntree Foundation 2000

Published for the Joseph Rowntree Foundation by The Policy Press

ISBN 1 86134 224 1

**Katy Bennett** is Lecturer and **Ray Hudson** is Professor and Chairman of the International Centre for Regional Regeneration and Social Development at the Department of Geography, University of Durham. **Huw Beynon** is Head of School and Director, Cardiff School of Social Sciences, at the University of Cardiff.

The **Joseph Rowntree Foundation** has supported this project as part of its programme of research and innovative development projects, which it hopes will be of value to policy makers, practitioners and service users. The facts presented and views expressed in this report are, however, those of the authors and not necessarily those of the Foundation.

The statements and opinions contained within this publication are solely those of the authors and contributors and not of The University of Bristol or The Policy Press. The University of Bristol and The Policy Press disclaim responsibility for any injury to persons or property resulting from any material published in this publication.

The Policy Press works to counter discrimination on grounds of gender, race, disability, age and sexuality.

Cover design by Qube Design Associates, Bristol.
Front cover, top centre photograph of Boughton Pumping Station's mission statement and top right photograph of Perthcelyn Estate kindly supplied by Katy Bennett.
Printed in Great Britain by Hobbs the Printers Ltd, Southampton

# Contents

# Acknowledgements

We are grateful to those who took part in this research, all of whom generously gave their time in spite of their busy schedules and lives. We would also like to thank our Advisory Board for their commitment to the project and helpful comments and advice. Also thanks to Sandra Bonney in the School of Social Sciences at Cardiff University for her help with the final draft of the manuscript and to David Hume and his colleagues in the Cartography Section of the Geography Department at Durham University for preparing the maps.

It is impossible individually to thank all the people involved in this research, but special thanks go to Phil Cope, Gary Foreman, Martin Hoban, Jill Owen, Carole Turner and Jenny Turner. Katy Bennett is also especially indebted to Bill and Leala Peacock and Viv Jensen with whom she stayed for three months while doing her fieldwork and who made her feel at home and also to Giles Mohan who is, as ever, supportive and spent most of his weekends on a train visiting former coalfields.

# List of tables and figures

# List of acronyms

| | |
|---|---|
| BCE | British Coal Enterprises |
| BCRS | Bryncynon Community Revival Strategy Ltd |
| BCSSS | British Coal Staff Superannuation Scheme |
| CCC | Coalfields Communities Campaign |
| CTF | Coalfields Task Force |
| DETR | Department of the Environment, Transport and the Regions |
| DTA | Development Trust Association |
| DTI | Department of Trade and Industry |
| EU | European Union |
| FDI | foreign direct investment |
| GDP | gross domestic product |
| MPS | Mineworkers' Pension Scheme |
| MWCDG | Mansfield Woodhouse Community Development Group |
| NCB | National Coal Board |
| NDC | Northern Development Company |
| NLCB | National Lottery Charities Board |
| NOMIS | National Online Manpower Information System |
| NPTCBC | Neath Port Talbot County Borough Council |
| NUM | National Union of Mineworkers |
| ONS | Office for National Statistics |
| RCT | Rhondda Cynon Taff |
| RCTCBC | Rhondda Cynon Taff County Borough Council |
| RDA | Regional Development Agency |
| RDC | Rural Development Commission |
| RTA | Residents' and Tenants' Association |
| SEU | Social Exclusion Unit |
| SMEs | small and medium-sized enterprises |
| SRB | Single Regeneration Budget |
| TTWA | Travel to Work Area |
| UDM | Union of Democratic Miners |
| VFR | Valleys Furniture Recycling |
| VIAE | Valleys Initiative for Adult Education |
| WDA | Welsh Development Agency |
| WEPE | Wales European Programme Executive |

# Coalfield decline

## Introduction

This is a story of industrial change and its social and spatial consequences. It examines the impact of these changes on communities and the people who live in them. It also considers public policy and local responses to industrial decline. It tells this story through the British coal industry and the places that have been built up around it. The industry's heyday was in the first two decades of the century when a million men were employed in and around the collieries. Subsequently, in the 1930s and then in the 1960s it experienced depression and contraction. In the 1980s and 1990s the industry went into rapid and near-terminal decline, with most of its 250,000 jobs disappearing. As such, it represents the most dramatic contemporary example of social transformation in Britain since the Second World War. The scale and intensity of it was recognised when the Labour government set up a special Task Force in 1997 to look at the consequences of coal mine closures. In its report it recognised the distinctive and unique character of the problems faced by the coalfields:

> ... we have been left in no doubt about the scale of deprivation and decline. But what makes the coalfields special is the context in which this decline has taken place. They have a unique combination of concentrated joblessness, physical isolation, poor infrastructure and severe health problems. (CTF, 1998, para 1.2)

The uniqueness of the problems of the coalfields derived in large part from the pace and intensity of the industry's decline. One measure of this can be seen in the ways that the coal districts increasingly became categorised as *rural*

districts. A change in nomenclature which recognised that their industrial employment had been removed. In places like East Durham, South Yorkshire and the South Wales valleys the local landscapes began to revert to those of a period before the footprint of mining was placed upon them.

The removal of the industrial footprint has had severe physical and emotional impacts upon the local mining communities. In some ways, their change of status has made them more picturesque as mines and slag heaps have been removed and landscaped. Nevertheless, they are not places where people purchase holiday homes. As Fred Redwood advised readers of *The Times*:

> Only those with personal knowledge of South Wales would consider buying in the valley towns. Many of the coal tips have been planted with greenery and forestry, but a cloud of post-industrialism still hangs over the region. Few would enjoy a second home here. (Redwood, 1999, p 29)

The same could be said of all the former coal districts, but the problem is most acute in South Wales where most of the coalmines closed with great rapidity in the mid-1980s. Ten years later, the parlous state of this area was discovered by John Redwood when Secretary of State for Wales. Discussing issues of 'rural poverty' in Mid Wales with a member of the Welsh Development Agency, he drew a contrast between these rural areas and the valleys:

> "When I look around housing estates [in the Welsh Valleys] I recognise poverty

and deprivation but when I look around me here – who could complain about living here, it is so beautiful."

Poverty in Mid Wales is much less obvious to the eye of the casual observer than in the de-industrialised valleys. So, while the old coalfield districts share much with the rural areas (isolation, low level of amenity and so on) they also differ from them in the density of their populations. In these and other ways they resemble many of the housing estates that ring the major urban centres. For these reasons – reasons which spring from a certain and important uniqueness – the collapse of the coal industry raises critical issues for public policy. This was well understood by the Coalfields Task Force (CTF) which, in its report, insisted that the public policy response to the situation had been inadequate:

> The contraction of the coal industry has been so rapid that mainstream government programmes have failed to readjust to offer an adequate level of support. Regeneration funding, which might have compensated, has been allocated on a basis that has tended not to reflect the particular nature of coalfield deprivation. (CTF, 1998, para 1.2)

The closure of the coalmines is an important story, for other reasons too – reasons that relate to the ways in which people's lives have been altered, disturbed and even destroyed by economic changes. It tells us about the dark side of industrial transformation that is often ignored in celebratory accounts of modernisation. It is this that is addressed in the vision outlined for these places by the Task Force. Its aim was:

> To set the framework which will empower coalfield communities affected by pit closures and job losses to create their own new start, forging their own sustainable and prosperous future, and to engage the active support of all partners, particularly the government, in its delivery. (CTF, 1998, p 1)

This, then, is a story that needs to be told and which, in its telling, reveals a lot about the world in which we currently live.

## Situating decline

Coalmining is an extractive industry and as such it is near to the land and has marked and visible impacts on the landscape that can remain long after the ending of mining. Coalmines are opened as coal reserves are discovered and mining them becomes both technologically feasible and economically viable. Coalfields were often quickly built up over short periods of time with rapid immigration in response to growing demand for coal. In these places, people learned to live with the risks associated with dangerous jobs in a world that was dominated by the coal owners. In the context of such a precarious existence, coalminers and their families created their own 'communities'. Relatively homogeneous, self-contained, and based on the village or town, these places owed their existence to coal and the coalmining occupations. They became communities through the activities of these people and the institutions (clubs, cooperative stores, chapels, trades unions, political parties) they created. This process of social construction took for granted that the mining of coal would be a continuous and ongoing process. At several points (in the 1950s and again in the 1970s) miners and their families had this belief reinforced by policy statements from governments and the National Coal Board. In the 1980s, however, it became clear that the assumption of the long-term stability of coalmining was unwarranted, and this was further proved in the 1990s. Over 200 coalmines closed in these two decades and the 20th century ended with news of yet another closure at Ellington and the vulnerability of still more mines. In this context coalfield places have had to face up to the economic and social consequences of this rapid process of job loss. Here, the personal and emotional impacts of change were deep ones, often experienced as hurt, anger and uncertainty.

Given that coalmining is an extractive industry, the decline and closure of particular mines and the communities dependent upon them is an unavoidable fact of life, albeit a regrettable one. Coalmines can close simply because the reserves of coal mined from them are exhausted; there are geological limits to production that cannot be avoided. There is a long history of mines closing because of the exhaustion of reserves, but this is not the only reason for closure.

## Table 1: Coalmining – long-term decline

| Year | Collieries | Employment (000s) | Output (million tonnes) |
|------|-----------|-------------------|-------------------------|
| 1947 | 958 | 704 | 187 |
| 1957 | 850 | 699 | 213 |
| 1967 | 483 | 456 | 177 |
| 1977 | 238 | 242 | 108 |
| 1987 | 101 | 115 | 90 |
| 1997 | 15 | 8 | 39 |

Over the last four decades the main reasons for coalmines closing in Great Britain have been economic and political rather than those of geology and exhaustion of reserves. This is not without a bitter irony as in the 1940s and 1950s, it seemed that nationalisation would provide a guaranteed future for coalmining – smoothing out the unavoidable changes in the industry in ways that would reduce the risks and uncertainties for miners, their families and communities. However, from the late 1950s it became clear that this was not to be the case. Changes in government energy policies and international energy markets have played a decisive role, with a particularly severe round of mine closures in the late 1960s. After a

temporary reprieve following the oil price rises of 1973/74 and 1979/80, the pace of decline accelerated again. The Thatcher government's assault on the nationalised industries made the coal industry vulnerable, especially after the defeat of the National Union of Mineworkers in the 1984/85 strike. This precipitated not simply further extensive colliery closures, but the privatisation of the industry and its rapid decline and disappearance from many of the 'traditional' heartlands of coalmining. The pace of decline was fierce. Following the ending of the 1984/85 strike, 171,400 miners were employed in 169 collieries of the public sector deep mining industry. By 1999, there were less than 10,000 miners employed by various employers in the remaining 14 coal mines (see Tables 1 and 2).

So intense was this process of contraction that all of the British coalfields were affected. In the early 1980s it was possible to imagine that closure would only affect the 'marginal' coalfields of South Wales, Kent, the North East and Scotland with production continuing unabated in the central coalfield areas of Nottingham and Yorkshire. This proved not to be the case. The 'central coalfield' was severely hit by closures with the local economies of towns like Barnsley and Mansfield being intensely affected. Nevertheless, the decline did prove to be most precipitous in the marginal

## Table 2: Surviving collieries (1999)

| Area | Mine | Operator | Potential output* |
|------|------|----------|-------------------|
| Scotland | Longannet | Mining Scotland | 2.0 |
| North East | Ellington | RJB Mining | 1.0 |
| Yorkshire | Hatfield | Hatfield Coal | 0.4 |
| | Kellingley | RJB Mining | 2.0 |
| | Maltby | RJB Mining | 2.0 |
| | Prince of Wales | RJB Mining | 2.2 |
| | Rossington | RJB Mining | 0.8 |
| | Selby Complex | RJB Mining | 11.0 |
| East Midlands | Harworth | RJB Mining | 2.0 |
| | Thoresby | RJB Mining | 2.0 |
| | Welbeck | RJB Mining | 2.0 |
| West Midlands | Daw Mill | RJB Mining | 2.3 |
| South Wales | Betws | Betws Anthracite | 0.1 |
| | Tower | Tower Anthracite | 1.0 |
| | | | 30.8 |

*Note:* * Million tonnes per year.

areas and because of this South Wales can perhaps be seen as prototypical of the impact that the closure of coal mines has on coal districts. Here (as in Kent) almost all of the remaining coal mines closed rapidly after the end of the miners' strike in 1984/85. In Durham, for example, some large mines remained open to be closed eight years later. As such the ramifications of closure have had more time to work themselves through in South Wales (see Table 3). By 1994 deep mining had ceased although subsequently a couple of small collieries – Betws and Tower – reopened, employing a few hundred men (see Chapter 3).

This was not just a case of localised economic decline but rather one of cultural crisis. The collapse of coalmining undermined a range of mechanisms of social regulation that were grounded in the politics of the workplace and the trades unions, but spread more widely into local society and politics. There was an acute sense of loss in places in which coalmines closed after decades of existence. This was typically accompanied by a period of grieving as people in these places tried to come to terms with the manifold implications of the precipitate ending of the economic *raison d'être* of their place.

While there was some recognition of the economic consequences of decline, there was much less acknowledgement of, and sensitivity to, the cultural and psychological dimensions of sudden closure. Central government established new organisations specifically charged with bringing about the economic regeneration of the former coalfields. This was in part in recognition of the severity of the effects of decline, in part a reflection of the political clout of the coalfields and their capacity to lobby for policies

specifically targeted at them. The first example of such an institution was British Coal Enterprises (BCE) – the job creation arm of the then nationalised coal industry – which was quickly making powerful (although contentious and contested) claims as to its success in providing new jobs and a fresh economic rationale for former coalfields. Soon a plethora of local enterprise agencies and job creation and training organisations were created to engage in the business of coalfield regeneration. Often it became difficult to disentangle the claims of competing job creation and training organisations with different institutions all seeming to want credit for the same new jobs and training opportunities. At the same time, rising rates of unemployment and of economic inactivity cast doubt on the veracity of such claims. This pattern of concentrated localised job loss and disputed claims as to the success of policies in creating alternative employment was shared across the coalfields.

## Coalfield devastation: causes and consequences

Most coalfield places were built up in rural locations and were completely dependent on the coalmining industry and their collieries as a source of paid employment for men. Local labour markets were often deliberately constructed so as to be dominated by this single industry, with government actively colluding in this process to ensure that there was little in the way of alternative employment. This was particularly the case under nationalisation. Alternative male jobs were intentionally kept out of the coalfields, and this continued to be the case until the 1960s. Such a mono-industrial structure meant that the effects of the mining industry extended beyond the mines and into community life, structuring political, social, household and leisure activities. As long as the mines remained open as significant sources of employment all was well. Once the mines began to close this old order was increasingly threatened.

This was particularly so in the 1980s, with the dominance of Thatcherism and its emphasis on markets rather than state provision, and the introduction of market-based criteria into what remained of the public sector. These, together with the pursuit of more restrictive fiscal

### Table 3: South Wales: mining employment (1947–94)

| Date | Collieries | Workforce |
|------|------------|-----------|
| 1947 | 214 | 114,930 |
| 1960 | 127 | 83,400 |
| 1970 | 52 | 38,000 |
| 1980 | 35 | 25,328 |
| 1990 | 3 | 1,200 |
| 1994 | 0 | 0 |

programmes, accelerated processes of economic globalisation and deindustrialisation. They were associated with a powerful push towards a 'post-industrial' economy within the UK based around services. Following the removal of government controls on capital export, major manufacturing companies shifted parts of their enterprises to other, cheaper locations outside of the UK, while national government promoted the City of London as a global financial centre. The result was to encourage the expansion of service sector industries in key growth areas – particularly London and the South East – and the decline and marginalisation of places dependent on heavy manufacturing and extractive industries (Hudson and Williams, 1995). These changes had particularly disastrous consequences for coal districts.

The neoliberal policy framework also encouraged competition between places for mobile public and private capital investment. All this was associated with a rhetoric that extolled the virtues of pro-activity and people and places solving their own problems. This had a profound effect on ideas of local regeneration. It also further exacerbated uneven development and increased the marginalisation of many places that lacked the capacities and resources needed to compete in the market place. Wealthier and economically strong areas, already endowed with greater institutional capacities and resources, tended to gain. Others were encouraged to emulate them. The coalfields suffered particularly badly in this competitive bidding environment, in relation both to the growth of new small and medium-sized enterprises (SMEs) and the attraction of major inward investment projects.

The coalfields still remain marginalised places, uncertain whether they are caught in a period of transformation, or just trapped on the long road of decline. Relatively well-paid, strongly unionised, often highly skilled male jobs have been replaced by a smaller number of poorly paid, unskilled and often part-time jobs (for example, in call centres). Many of these jobs are taken by women, often the wives and daughters of ex-miners. Despite strong claims about the creation of new jobs (see for example, BCE, 1996), such places are experiencing high levels of economic inactivity (at least in the formal sector) and the increasing feminisation of their workforces. This has gone alongside spiralling problems of petty crime, substance abuse, a decline in their local facility and service provision, poor housing conditions and poor health – the hallmarks of dereliction and decline and all inextricably linked to growing poverty. While some have prospered, the cumulative impact of all these changes on individuals and their communities has often been devastating.

# 2

# Governing communities: policies and institutions for regenerating places

## Introduction

While there are differences between them, it is clear that the coalfields share common problems. Because of this they have found ways of working together to press their shared cause. The formation of the Coalfields Communities Campaign was an important development. Its political mobilisation was critical in convincing the European Union (EU) to recognise the special case of coalfields. This, together with other political organisations representing coalfield interests within Europe, resulted in the establishment of the EU's RECHAR programme. Over two phases (1990-93, 1994-97 – extended to 1999 in some areas), RECHAR provided a special programme of assistance for the regeneration of coalfields. Within the UK, the creation of the Coalfields Task Force was another example of this clout. As an intervention in the politics of industrial regeneration it was unique. While other places experienced industrial decline and social deprivation, none of them received attention and support on a comparable scale.

## Sustainable growth: economic development and social and physical regeneration

The new Labour government has developed a distinctive approach to issues of regeneration and economic development. While these are still seen as separate issues, they are also recognised to be dependent on one another if regional growth is to be achievable. In the government's view, economic development and regeneration have been treated as isolated issues in the past. As a result:

... opportunities for each to reinforce the other – for economic growth to include those on the margins of society, or for physical and social regeneration to foster the conditions in which business can flourish – have been lost. (DETR, 1997, p 18)

A central aim of the 1997 White Paper is to connect economic development and regeneration, but with economic development as the driving force, spearheading social and physical regeneration.

Similarly:

... finding ways to integrate economic, social and environmental objectives to ensure a better quality of life for everyone – now and for generations to come – is at the heart of what has come to be called 'sustainable development'. (DETR, 1997, p 40)

As such, for New Labour sustainability depends on economic development. The White Paper argues that:

Under-performance in an economy risks putting greater pressure on the environment: firms are reluctant to invest in plant and technology to reduce or eliminate pollution; business failures increase the amount of land falling derelict or subject to degradation; and the temptation to use up our 'capital' resources (such as land and other natural resources), rather than employing more sensitive and sustainable forms of development, can become overwhelming. (DETR, 1997, pp 39-40)

The consequences of economic under-performance – high unemployment and low incomes – can, in turn, lead to further degradation of public spaces and housing.

Basically, for New Labour, unless the mainstream economy is working, regeneration is considered to be impossible. At the same time, however, its policy agenda has created renewed space for consideration of issues of poverty and social exclusion, communities and regional devolution as central to the achievement of sustainable economic development and not simply as a consequence of it. The emphasis on the mainstream economy as the key to regeneration is very much the thinking behind the establishment of Regional Development Agencies (RDAs), which are charged with developing and implementing regional economic strategies and providing a coherent focus for sustainable economic development (and social and physical regeneration).

## 'Joined-up government' and area-based initiatives

In 1997, the Coalfields Task Force visited coalfield areas across England to listen to the issues, concerns and problems of local people and the organisations and agencies working with coalfield communities. The Task Force produced its report in 1998 and, in its response, the government announced a 10-year programme to combat deprivation in the former coalfield communities. Over the period 1999-2002, in excess of £350 million of additional money (see Table 4) will combine with the

better targeting of the £3 billion already going to local authorities with responsibilities for coalfield areas to give a significant boost to coalfield regeneration. Two new coalfield institutions have been established to help deliver this programme. These are the Coalfields Regeneration Trust (a Great Britain-wide charitable body independent of government and a potential forum for the exchange of good practice and the monitoring of government programmes) and a Coalfield Enterprise Fund (which will support coalfield-based firms with high growth potential). Other potential sources of this new investment include Round 5 of the Single Regeneration Budget (SRB) (the Bidding Guidance has highlighted the needs of the coalfields) and the Housing Investment Programme, which is to target coalfield housing with an extra £28 million over the next three years. The government also addressed the issue of the low share of Lottery funding that had been distributed to coalfield areas.

This initiative was also linked to another major innovation in governance developed by New Labour. This involved a series of 'cross-cutting' area-based initiatives, focused on the most deprived areas that continued to be bypassed by mainstream programmes. The Cabinet Office's Social Exclusion Unit's 1998 Report, *Bringing Britain together*, looked at the problems facing the poorest neighbourhoods and at ways of alleviating them through two programmes – Sure Start (to support young children in poor neighbourhoods) and the New Deal for Communities. In addition to these – and reminiscent of policy responses to localised poverty in the 1960s and early 1970s – the government introduced the idea of *zoning* to

**Table 4: Future government investment in the coalfields (£m) (1999-2002)**

|  | 1999-2000 | 2000-01 | 2001-02 |
| --- | --- | --- | --- |
| English Partnerships coalfields programme | 64 | 69 | 63 |
| Coalfields regeneration trust | 30 | 10 | 5 |
| Coalfield enterprise fund | 5 | 5 | 5 |
| Coalfields housing | 8 | 10 | 10 |
| SRB partnerships | 10 | 20 | 40 |
| Total | 117 | 114 | 123 |

*Source:* DETR (1998, p 7)

encourage new ways of working. These include Health Action Zones, Education Action Zones and Employment Zones.

The main aim of such area-based initiatives is to devolve their ownership, control and design, with the intention of allowing local partnerships to develop innovative and flexible ways of helping their places and the people who live in them. This devolution to local partnerships represents a major transformation in the mode of governance in the UK. In this new framework, the state abrogates responsibility for dealing with a range of social problems, passing it on to local partnerships. The promotion of genuine and organic local partnerships with stronger local involvement is therefore critical to this new pattern of governance. As such, government agendas are both informed and reinforced by reports like that of the Coalfields Task Force which, incidentally, dedicates a chapter to 'The importance of partnership' stating that "effective partnerships are the key to successful regeneration" (CTF, 1998, para 4.1).

## Partnerships

Unsurprisingly our research revealed that a large number of partnerships of different types operated across the English and Welsh coalfields. In some instances there are overlapping webs of partnerships. This was particularly evident in East Durham and Mansfield (one of the two districts which we examined in considerable detail). These partnerships involved government bodies, quangos, the community and voluntary organisations and occasionally private sector utility companies (see for example, East Durham Task Force, 1997). However, private sector involvement is almost always marginal. Our research findings indicate that coalfield partnerships are almost entirely based on the activities of public sector and voluntary bodies, all of which are strapped for cash. Occasionally the private sector plays a role, but, in our experience, this is rare and limited to some of the privatised utilities.

Nevertheless, most organisations and agencies involved in partnerships on the coalfields highlight their positive role in developing a strategic framework for delivering and coordinating regeneration initiatives and programmes. In practice, however, the main

motive of partnership is instrumental – that is, to access external funding in competition with other places. Such sources of funding have become increasingly important with the erosion of local authorities' financial powers and resources through budget cuts and capping. For the coalfield communities, external funding sources include the European Structural Funds, the SRB and the National Lottery Charities Board (NLCB). Twenty per cent of SRB Round 5 funding is targeted at significant pockets of deprivation, including coalfields. Its bidding criteria heavily emphasises the need for partnership working. Partnerships, then, may reflect the eligibility criteria of government funding regimes rather than the particular needs and aspirations of localities.

Despite devolving responsibility for their regeneration to localities, power is largely still centrally held. While the EU has for some time sought to tackle economic and social issues together, encouraging local partnerships between private and public sectors and directly funding places to realise their regeneration initiatives, this has not always been (and arguably is still not) the case for the UK. Indeed, it seems this way to some of those involved on behalf of the government. A representative of one regional Government Office told us that while the EU "has always laid great emphasis on partnership working, the UK Government resisted and wanted a fairly tight grip on the funds". While government thinking has shifted to favour partnership working, its 'tight grip' is a recurring theme. The new English RDAs set up (outside of London) in April 1999 were "to co-ordinate the work of regional and local partners in areas such as training, investment, regeneration and business support" (DETR, 1997, p 9). These non-departmental governmental bodies have taken on the regeneration work previously carried out by organisations such as the Northern Development Company. They have taken on the regional responsibilities of English Partnerships, the regeneration programmes of the Rural Development Commission and the administration of the SRB. Part of each RDA's remit is to draw up a Regional Economic Strategy, which is to enhance and support national policies in ways that meet regional needs. While RDAs will be monitored by, and expected to respond to, Regional Chambers, which bring together representatives from local authorities and other regional partners, their strategies are constrained and shaped by government agendas and guidance. Although the Coalfields Task Force argued that partnerships are "a powerful and cost effective vehicle for identifying programmes that reflect the specific needs of local people" (CTF, 1998, para 4.3), it is clear that central government is driving the 'vehicle'. As the DETR put it:

> It follows that in defining functions and structures we must ensure that RDAs have the freedom to decide for themselves how they can most effectively operate and meet the objectives we set them. (1997, p 43)

However, the English RDAs lack both constitutional legitimacy and the resources needed effectively to pursue devolved regeneration strategies. This limits their capacity to discharge both their general responsibilities for regional development and the specific responsibilities that they have been given for coalfield regeneration. As such they often find themselves cast as followers of Westminster's agenda rather than agenda-setters in their own right. Something of the frustration of this came through in one public meeting when the representative of one RDA turned to the civil servants on the platform and pleaded: "trust us more".

This situation contrasts with developments in Scotland and Wales. There, devolution has been linked to the formation of an elected Scottish Parliament and Welsh Assembly. These bodies have powers to set policy priorities and the funds to carry some of them out. In both Scotland and Wales the new elected bodies will be able to build upon the work of development agencies established in the mid-1970s, with budgets greater than those currently being given to the new English agencies, which they have inherited. As one of the coal districts that we investigated in depth is in South Wales (Rhondda Cynon Taff) and the position of the English Regions is more likely to evolve along the Welsh lines of an Assembly than the Scottish model of a Parliament, the governance arrangements in Wales are of particular relevance. The new Assembly occupies a pivotal position in a complicated system of governance that extends in one direction upwards to the EU and in the other down to local authorities and community groups in Wales, while sitting in a sometimes uneasy relationship with the UK Parliament in Westminster.

## Community empowerment?

Partnership working is closely linked with the idea of community empowerment as "it is widely recognised today that the community must be the key focus of regeneration programmes if they are to be effective" (CTF, 1998, para 5.1). The Coalfields Task Force goes on to highlight the issues that need to be addressed for a community to become empowered, focusing on education, employment, debt, crime and health. It recognises that the coalfields are made up of communities that were once strong, but have been weakened by the devastation of the mining industry. Economic collapse has stretched and, at times, ruptured the social fabric. The New Labour government is anxious to address this issue. In future schemes funded by SRB Round 5, the government wants to raise community aspirations. It 'wishes to see' up to 10% of its resources being dedicated to community capacity building so that every former coalfield community is able "to take an active role in a coalfields Regeneration Partnership" (DETR, 1998, p 13).

This is a significant development in the pattern of governance in the UK. For partnerships to work, there is a need for "a more collaborative, wide-ranging approach" (Welsh Office, 1998, p 39) that is dependent on community empowerment. Thus

> We want to encourage people to help themselves. We want to enable communities to set their own agendas so that individuals can help themselves. (Welsh Office, 1998, p 39)

The government's response document to the Coalfields Task Force report noted that:

> ... where SRB coalfield partnerships are felt to be weak, the most common problem is lack of genuine community involvement.... (DETR, 1998, p 13)

As such, the government's position is, that for its strategies to be realised, partnerships need to include, and work with, empowered communities.

Nonetheless, this leaves a number of critical questions unanswered. Is the main problem in partnership formation lack of capacity, or is it (as a number of people involved in community initiatives told us with some force) a lack of money and other resources? Who is to be empowered? Are all people in a place to be empowered equally? Will partnerships that began life as temporary instrumental coalitions in search of funding evolve into more long-standing organic entities – or simply fade away and die once the money runs out? The answers to these questions are of immense practical importance for those living in the coal districts.

# 3

# Two coalfield places

## Introduction

The research reported here focuses on two places: Rhondda Cynon Taff (RCT) in South Wales and Mansfield in North Nottinghamshire (see Figure 1). In these two places, the strategies of the community sector were explored. We did this by spending time in the two communities and by one of us (Katy Bennett) living in each of them for three months. In these ways we visited people in their homes, met them in the pubs and clubs, attended their meetings and talked with local activists, often in an informal setting. In this, participant observation was our main research approach. This allowed detailed involvement in and access to over 30 local community initiatives (see Appendix A) as well as more formal interviews with key activists. These techniques yielded a wealth of in-depth information and important comparative data. In order to establish the reliability of our materials, each of the community initiatives was contacted to confirm the factual details in our account. Nonetheless, it is important to stress that these results should be considered as preliminary rather than definitive insofar as they are based on detailed research in only two of many coal districts.

The two districts have long histories of coalmining and both have experienced severe loss of jobs through colliery closure. However, the pattern of decline has been different in each case. In RCT almost all the mines had closed by the mid-1980s. In 1980 the area was still associated strongly with coalmining. In the valleys of the Rhonda, the Cynon and the Taff pits like Fernhill, Lady Windsor, Tymawr Lewis Merthyr, Deep Dufryn and Merthyr Vale were producing coal and employing large numbers of men. By 1999 only the Tower Colliery, high up at the north end of the Cynon Valley, remained open. This had previously closed and after a considerable struggle reopened as a successful and innovative miners' cooperative. In Mansfield, the pattern of colliery closure has been more drawn out but nonetheless painful. Mansfield was a major mining centre and, in 1980, 15 collieries that made up the North Nottingham division of the National Coal Board ringed the town. These included significant mines like Bevercotes and Welbeck, Blidworth and Bilsthorpe and Ollerton. Unlike South Wales, some of these mines survived into the mid-1990s. But then Bilsthorpe, Clipstone and Harworth closed down. In 1999, Welbeck, to the north of the town, was all that remained of a once powerful coalmining region.

The districts vary in their settlement patterns. Rhondda Cynon Taff (see Figure 2) has a largely rural landscape with its relatively small settlements strung out in ribbons along the valley sides. This area became historically heavily dependent on the mining industry and almost synonymous with coal. In contrast, the closure of pits in Mansfield (see Figure 3) occurred in the context of larger losses of jobs from manufacturing industries, notably clothing and textiles. Some of the basic socioeconomic characteristics of these two districts and the wider regions within which they are situated are summarised in Tables 5, 6 and 7.

**Figure 1: Two coalfield places**

**Figure 2: Rhondda Cynon Taff, South Wales**

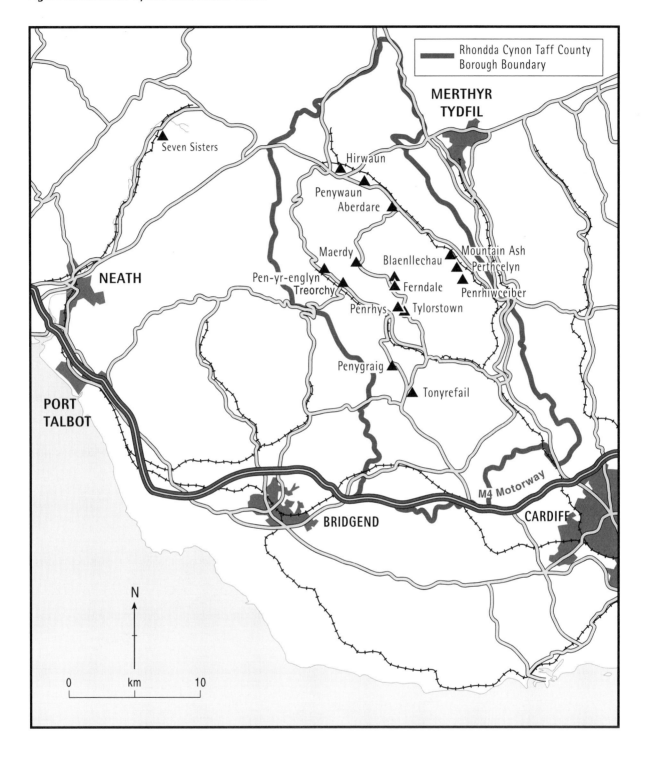

**Figure 3: Mansfield, North Nottinghamshire**

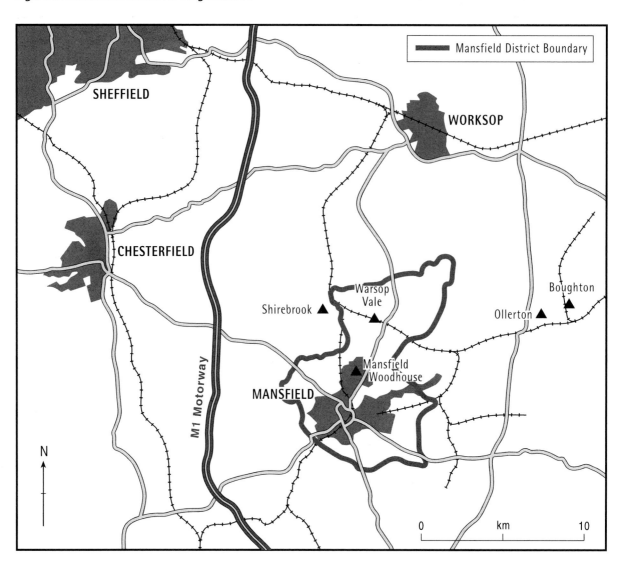

**Table 5: Earnings in coalfield areas (April 1997)**

|  | Average gross weekly earnings (£) | Percentage earning less than £250 per week | Highest weekly earnings of lowest decile (£) |
|---|---|---|---|
| Great Britain | 367.20 | 31.7 | 175.30 |
| North Nottinghamshire | 322.30 | 43.2 | 158.60 |
| Mid Glamorgan | 320.40 | 41.2 | 166.30 |

*Source:* ONS (1997)

**Table 6: Labour market and demographic characteristics in two coal districts**

|  | Population change, 1981–96 (%) | Unemployment rate January 1997 claimant count (%) | 'real' (%) | Standardised Mortality Ratio |
|---|---|---|---|---|
| UK | +4.3 | 7.1* | 14.2* | 100 |
| Mansfield | +1.4 | 8.4 | 21.1 | 105 |
| RCT | +0.7 | 9.2 | 28.0 | 115 |

*Note:* * Data refer to Great Britain.
*Sources:* NOMIS; Beatty et al (1997); ONS (1998)

**Table 7: Employment in manufacturing (1996–97)**

|  | Total in employment (000s) | Manufacturing as % of total |
|---|---|---|
| UK | 26,462 | 19.1 |
| Nottinghamshire | 441 | 23.5 |
| RCT | 95 | 30.7 |

*Source:* ONS (1998)

Sectoral changes in these local economies have been associated with rising numbers of women working and increases in part-time work. In Mansfield, for example, there has been:

... an increase in part-time working. In 1981 41.6% of female employment in Mansfield District was part-time. By 1995 this had risen to 49.9%. The total number of female part-time employees increased by 9% over the period. (Mansfield District Council, 1998, Section 3.4)

Moreover these changes have been associated with the creation of a low wage economy:

... wage costs are significantly below the national average and are therefore very competitive. The average gross weekly earnings of employees in Mansfield District (across occupations) is £268.50 compared with £306.80 for Nottinghamshire as a whole and with £351.70 nationally. (quoted in Mansfield District Council, 1998, Section 3.3)

These changes mesh with, and are a direct consequence of, the types of formal strategies for regeneration that have been developed on the coalfields.

## Regeneration via selling coalfield places to the private sector?

In these two places, local authorities and other agencies faced with the problem of industrial decline have been trying to regenerate their local economies. To investigate these issues, we conducted a series of in-depth interviews with key actors involved in regeneration programmes in these and other places across the English and Welsh coalfields (see Appendix B). Most generally this involved an attempt to attract investment and money from outside the districts. In this process, images of the areas were projected through glossy brochures, CD-roms and websites in an attempt to attract the maximum amount of private sector inward investment (see Figures 4 and 5). This was done in the context of fierce competition at international, inter-regional and intra-regional levels as places vied with each other for jobs.

The great reliance on attracting inward investment to former coalfield places perhaps reflects a realistic assessment of the difficulties of successfully implementing policies to encourage the formation and growth of SMEs there. These difficulties arise not because people lack entrepreneurial qualities but rather because they are acutely aware of the difficulties of seeking to establish new small firms in places that are profoundly economically depressed, and behave very rationally in response to this realisation (Rees and Thomas, 1991). There are claims that regions such as the North East of England have been successful in attracting direct foreign investment (CTF, 1998, paras 2.12-2.13) but little of this has been in the former coalfields. In the words of the former MEP for Cynon Valley, Wayne David, when we interviewed him in 1997:

> "... we have seen ... a lot of inward investment coming into not just Cardiff but on the M4 corridor generally in South Wales – American investment, Japanese, Korean, especially with LG in Newport. And that is in sharp contrast to what is happening in the valleys. The valleys have failed to attract either any substantial new investment into the area or actually succeeded in creating any indigenous growth."

While this exclusion from inward investment is perhaps most pronounced in RCT, it is by no means limited to that area. More generally, there is a weight of evidence suggesting that the policies of reliance on inward investment have been, at best, partially successful (Hudson, 1995; Lovering, 1996). Regional and local economies remain vulnerable and this vulnerability can even be reinforced by their success in winning foreign direct investment (FDI). This was evident in 1998, with the drastic curtailment of the proposed new LG complex in south Wales and the closure of the Fujitsu and Siemens factories in North East England. Micro-chips no longer seemed to be such an attractive feature on the economic regeneration menu. This highlighted a more general point. The claims that FDI was no longer in the form of branch plants that were vulnerable 'global outposts' but now took the form of 'performance plants', embedded in their region of destination, began to look rather threadbare.

More generally, there is evidence that the regeneration strategies of the formal sector have failed and are failing former coalfield places in terms of creating jobs to replace those lost as a result of colliery closures. For example, strong claims have been made about policy successes by BCE, set up in the wake of the miners' strike in the 1980s to bring alternative employment to coalfield areas. Shortly before it came to the end of its life, BCE stated in its *1996 Annual Report* (BCE, 1996) that it had assisted in the creation of 130,000 jobs on the coalfields in the previous decade. This claim is partly supported by the research of Fothergill and Guy (1994) insofar as it shows that in the decade from March 1984 to March 1994 coalfield districts gained manufacturing jobs in contrast to the national trend. Nevertheless, they indicate that net gain in total employment in the coalfields of England and Wales was only 16,000, compared with the claim by BCE that it had assisted in creating 106,000 jobs on the coalfield over this decade and with a known loss in coalmining employment of 228,000. This was, then, at best, a limited and partial transformation of the coalfield labour markets. And such a picture of partial and uneven transformation resonates strongly with the experiences of many residents of the coal districts. It also helps explain the projection of a very different sort of image of the former coalfields to that outlined above – that is, one of areas of continuing economic crisis and social dislocation that need continuing and enhanced levels of public sector support rather than one of successfully transformed areas built around new and modern economic activities.

**Figure 4: Rhondda Cynon Taff brochure – 'A vision for business success'**

*Source:* RCTCBC (1998)

**Figure 5: Mansfield District Council's 'Business Guide' brochure**

*Source:* Mansfield District Council (1998)

## Survival via public sector funding?

The limitations of top-down and private sector-led regeneration strategies are acknowledged in the ways in which local authorities in these two areas seek to attract public sector funding. They do so by projecting images of their areas as blighted by continuing levels of high and long-term unemployment and poverty. In some ways these problems are exacerbated by regeneration policies as companies locate within them, enticed by low wages as cheap labour has often featured as part of the attraction of such areas to inward investors. 'Grey literature', such as various reports relating to the EU's RECHAR Programme and Single Programming Documents seeking EU structural funding, typically focus on two themes when seeking to demonstrate the problems of these places: their physical aspects and the people who live there.

Considerable emphasis is placed on their peripherality, reinforced by inadequate road and rail infrastructure. Mansfield and RCT both emphasise the 'unsatisfactory' east–west road and rail links, with existing transport infrastructure reflecting past mining and old, heavy industrial demands and, in the case of RCT, the particular topography of the place. For Mansfield, this is particularly pertinent

> ... with the change in emphasis on economic activity favouring the East Coast – particularly Harwich and Felixstowe – together with the opening of the Channel Tunnel. (East Midlands Objective 2 Area, 1997, p 24)

Inadequate infrastructure creates difficulties for many people in accessing employment opportunities and services, particularly for those on low income and with no car in circumstances in which public transport provision is poor, infrequent and/or unreliable and/or expensive.

Low levels of personal mobility, especially when combined with a relatively high percentage of home ownership (redundant miners often spent a large part of their 'redundancy money' paying off their mortgages), locks people into these localities. Their subsequent low incomes combine with the ongoing effects of the mining legacy to exert a downward pressure on the local environment and on the condition of the housing stock. Such environmental degradation

and resulting downward pressure on rental values and rates of return deter speculative private sector developers from investing in such places.

Both districts emphasise the grave levels of registered unemployment and the high numbers of ex-miners on sickness-related benefits (see also Beatty et al, 1997). The labour market legacies of the collapse of coalmining extend beyond unemployment, however. Coalfield economies developed particular occupational and skill structures, which have left a legacy of people lacking skills, or possessing skills that are specific to coalmining and non-transferrable to other activities. The point is made forcibly with respect to South Wales but is more generally relevant throughout the coal districts:

> The skills and qualifications of the workforce in the area reflect the history of coal mining. Almost half the RECHAR area's males of working age have manual occupations, just over a quarter of these in skilled employment.... Fewer than one in six males and females holds a professional managerial or technical position. There is therefore a limited pool of people with experience in skilled technical or managerial work. Former employees of the coal industry often have skills which are specific to mining and which cannot be transferred. (South Wales Coalfield RECHAR 2 Programme, 1994, p 15)

The impact of considerable job losses through pit closures has been further intensified in both places by the loss of jobs in other sectors of the economy. Mansfield TTWA, with its clothing and textile industries, suffered "dramatic reductions in their employment levels" (East Midlands Objective 2 Area, 1997, p 5). In addition to reductions and job losses in manufacturing, which is still seen as a significant sector of employment for both places, growth in service industries is well below the national average. Despite this, the service sector is still by far the biggest source of jobs and the largest employment growth sector. These are not, however, the most desirable service sector jobs. There is a virtual absence of well-paid jobs in financial services for example – service sector employment on the coalfields is predominantly made up of poorly paid jobs with little skill content, many of them part-time.

All of this is having detrimental effects on the households. In Nottingham for example:

> Research carried out by Nottingham University following the major pit closures in 1992 to 1994, indicated changes in lifestyle which have a negative impact on health. This was particularly in the area of relationship breakdown ... Nottingham has the highest number of couples who file for divorce. The rise in families classified as high risk for child protection issues, the rise in drug misuse, particularly amongst young people, and the high proportion of burglary and robbery crime committed by young people are significant manifestations of these changes. (North Nottinghamshire Director of Public Health, 1997, p 21)

Poor health is well documented, especially in RCT (see Table 6). Not only are there high levels of illness associated with coalmining, but there is also evidence of impaired health caused by job loss and its associated problems such as poverty and stress.

## Everyday life: experiences from the grass roots

Both Mansfield and RCT share an industrial rural landscape set against sometimes picturesque rural backdrops: Mansfield is on the edge of Sherwood Forest, RCT is in mountainous landscape typical of the Welsh Valleys. For people who live there, however, these surroundings form a backdrop to the hectares of derelict land which testify to the world that has been lost. The housing in these towns and villages is at best in poor condition, at worst empty, boarded up, sometimes burnt out, regularly covered in graffiti. Here the people deal with an ongoing process of declining local services and facilities. Many of the people we talked with felt trapped in these places, unable to look out and beyond them. Often they were overwhelmed with a sense of hopelessness and despair. Often they looked back to the time when the pits were working and they compared this with the present. No doubt these reflections were selective and partial. Nevertheless, what is clear is that they were constructed around the mining industry, an industry that provided reasonably

well-paid jobs and supported their daily lives, in their communities and households with a degree of certainty. These memories of a past defined through a strong community identity are a crucial part of these places. They also serve to sharpen people's understanding of contemporary life and the social divisions within it.

Much of the pain experienced in these ex-mining communities is patterned around generational conflict. Young people feel alienated from older generations who are able to remember their place in terms of the community life of the past. With their designer labelled track suits and trainers, these young people typically define themselves as different from, and often in opposition to, older generations. Groups of adults made up of retired men wearing suits trudge their weekly patterns with predictable regularity. For them, walking and commenting on accustomed aspects of the local environment make up central parts of the day. They often comment on the young people and their different values and the fact that "they don't know what work is". The irony of this statement is often lost in its utterance. Older women meet up on Sunday nights to play bingo, unemployed fathers with pushchairs and carrier bags, mums and dads trying to make a living, trying to survive. All of these people, although different from one another form part of an 'other' from which young people seek to differentiate themselves – in whatever ways are open to them. This is exemplified in the following extract from *a bad name?*, a book written by seven young women who live on the Fernhill estate on the outskirts of Mountain Ash:

> This is a typical weekend. There is nothing for us to do, so we all go up the mountain, because it's out of sight from the police. We just get stoned and pissed. It might sound boring to everyone else but it's one of the most exciting things we do. All week up Fernhill, there is nothing to do, apart from the 'drop-in' which is only on a Monday. It's only been running since September 1997. Fernhill is clearly going downhill. When the community centre first opened we used to have children's bingo, keep-fit night, adult's bingo and now all they have is adult's bingo. So that's why we have turned to drugs and drink – for excitement. (Fernhill Estate Young Women, 1999)

Older generations are concerned about, and sometimes fearful of, young people and behaviour that they see as socially unacceptable and threatening to their notions of 'community'.

---

### Who *cares?*

is there anybody who cares today?
why children are left on their own
to play
they are able to do and have what
they like
to know what terrible things go on in the world
it just does not make sense, it is
a terrible sight
is there anyone who
cares?

their fathers will lose their jobs
there is not enough money to go
around
well, what happens then?
their mams will have to go and look
for a job
the children are left
on their own, the unlucky ones that is
the little ones, the big ones, to roam all
alone
isn't there anyone around who cares?

they make excuses, the people at the
top
they say that it is not their fault,
come on
we all know that is a lot of rot
what is going to happen to these children?
will they ever have a chance to
grow up as they should?
what sense does all this make?
isn't there anybody
who cares?
if our children grow up not knowing a
thing
what happens then, come on, for all our
children's sakes
please someone out there have the guts
please care
and get us all out of this mess

do you
not care?

(BCRSP, 1999)

---

Within both places there are pockets of intense deprivation, sometimes (wrongly) perceived as 'dangerous places' from which members of the wider community seek to separate themselves. These places are often particular housing estates, built on the edge of villages or towns dominated by a landscape of public sector owned, poor condition houses. In the Welsh Valleys they are frequently situated on top of the mountains that separate the valleys. Not only are they physically separated from the valley bottom communities, but they are also visually distinctive, with housing styles that are different from valley bottom terraces. Penrhys Housing Estate, situated on top of a mountain that divides Rhondda Fawr and Rhondda Fach, is an example of this with its 1960s built 'half' houses with high backs, low fronts and sloping roofs dominating the landscape. Perthcelyn and Fernhill, which overlook the Cynon Valley, are further examples of housing estates set on mountains (see Figure 6). It is easy to pass these estates without knowing their existence, because they are set back from roads and are hidden by other housing.

The traditional working-class communities of the valley floor, which are associated with the remnants of industrial activity, are thus separated from the marginalised working class of the hilltop housing estates (Adamson and Jones, 1996). Both are distinct from the new working-class communities living in newly-built private housing developments. *a bad name?* describes the divisions between hilltop estates and newly built estates:

> The difference between Forest View and Fernhill is that Fernhill is noisy and Forest View is peaceful. The houses are different – Forest View's are mortgaged and Fernhill's are council-owned. Forest View houses are built nicely. Fernhill's houses are shaped exactly the same as each other.

> Fernhill is fenced away from Forest View. This shows how Fernhill people and those of Forest View are differently classed – Fernhill the lower and Forest View the higher.

Littering is not a problem for Forest View. It's all clean and tidy, probably because they actually use their bins. Fernhill is full of rubbish because bins are used for fires.

Some Fernhill people go to the site and steal building materials. They resent the new snotty houses. (Fernhill Estate Young Women, 1999)

Even within such estates some parts are defined as worse than others, such as Willow Terrace on Perthcelyn Estate, which houses people that are seen to have the biggest problems. Clearly housing allocation policies and housing managers' perceptions of 'good' and 'bad' tenants are critical in this process of sifting and sorting people into different types of houses and places. The Residents' and Tenants' Association of Perthcelyn attempts to protect its members and their families by playing a role in determining who can move where when vacancies arise. For some, there are places on the estate where they will not live, or are fearful

of visiting. These places are controlled by drug dealers and petty criminals, who threaten and target those who give their names to the police. Pockets of deprivation are not only contained within estates. In Mansfield Town, entire streets, such as Brownlow Road and Bould Street, are dominated by vandalised, boarded up and graffitied housing, with gardens heaped with rubbish.

There are also contemporary geographical divisions that reflect past events within the coal districts. In North Nottinghamshire, there are still rifts that divide the National Union of Mineworkers and those who broke away to join the Union of Democratic Mineworkers following the 1984/85 miners' strike. In Ollerton, one drinking establishment is dominated by one union and another by the other, for example. This is common and it will remain so. Stories about the strike are still told, as it remains a fixed and strong memory for most people living in the place. The social geography of such places is deeply marked by past conflict and without doubt this is most marked in Nottinghamshire.

**Figure 6: Looking down onto the Cynon Valley from Perthcelyn Estate**

# 4

# Coalfield community initiatives

## Introduction

Formal sector top-down policies have failed to provide sufficient alternative employment – as we have demonstrated in Chapter 3 – in former coalfield places. This failure, however, creates scope for community initiatives to do regenerative work in those places in which formal sector attempts have not succeeded in attracting jobs. These community initiatives have many things in common. Tackling the problems of a particular place is a common theme. So too is that of accessing funding, something they must face and overcome if they are to realise their objectives. The demands of funding structures cause further apparent similarities in objectives and outputs, affecting the character and range of the services that they offer. They produce a tendency towards a sameness and serial repetition in services offered. Moreover, while initiatives claim that they are community controlled and led, and aim to be self-sustainable, this is not always the case. Furthermore, the concept of 'community control' is far from unambiguous – who in a 'community' controls what, for whom?

## Concepts of community and community development

Communities are a core concern of this research but the concept of community is a shifting and slippery one, not least because different people construct the concept in particular ways to suit their own purposes. Government documents make repeated reference to 'community', especially in relation to the coalfields where they want "every former coalfield community to take an active role in a coalfields Regeneration Partnership" (DETR, 1998, p 13). The notion of community then is central to public funding structures such as SRB Round 5 where the government "wishes to see up to 10% of resources per scheme going to community capacity building activity" (DETR, 1998, p 13). Following this, key informants, representing the formal sector, deploy concepts of 'community' in policy design and implementation. For these policy makers and those involved in the delivery of policies it is used as a 'third way' between the state and the market, between the state and the individual, and it is moulded into meaning a rejuvenated civil society. This then can be used to legitimise strategies that distract attention from central and local government funding policies to focusing it on 'locally made' decisions and choices.

In contrast, for people living in places they have known for most of their lives, 'community' denotes a past time when everyone knew each other, when doors were never locked, and people helped each other and stuck together. These ideas are most often grounded in a secure sense of place and a sense of belonging. In many ways, their insecurities about what is happening to them now and the changes that they are experiencing in their places is conveyed through a perceived loss of community.

Both these uses of community are, however, static cross-sections, often 'stills' forced upon an ongoing process. For people in a place, the community as a 'thing' of the past is a distant snapshot (but one with a rosy glow rather than a sepia tint) of an evolving process. For those involved in those organisations formally charged with community regeneration, and therefore, talking about community from the outside, it is a thing to be used normatively, something to propel people along a chosen path. As such, hopeful visions can be layered upon it. With luck, 'community' can be created through repetition of the word.

A group of people (community workers, community initiative coordinators and community development officers) has the task of bridging official discourses of 'community' and the lived experiences of people in places going through dramatic structural changes. These people spend their working lives in what is often termed the community sector (which better reflects their expertise than the use of the term 'voluntary sector'). Here they are a constitutive part of a very messy process that encompasses individuals with different and perhaps competitive and incompatible needs and priorities. Individuals who differentiate themselves from one another according to who they are, where they live, what they do and where they do (or do not) go to work, to shop, to enjoy themselves and so on. These activities can be seen to be constitutive of a 'community'. However, there are people who fail to engage with any of these processes in a meaningful way. Such people feel alien from, and fall outside of, any notion of community building. Many of these people do not feel they belong. Constructions of community in their nature both include and exclude.

What this points to is that the notion of community often masks issues of inequality and questions of power. In fact, some would argue that this has been one of the main functions of the term. Given this, the development of official policies and notions of 'community empowerment' raises some important questions about whom, in these communities, is benefiting from empowerment? Who feels empowered to do what? It also invites the question: Who benefits? It might not benefit those people who fall outside quite particular conceptions and definitions of communities. It might not reach the socially excluded. The construction of community is an inherently contested process, with some people failing to engage with it and others actively excluded from it whether they wish to be or not. As a result, often only particular individuals will be empowered by policies intended to empower whole communities.

Not only is the concept of community confusing, but so too is the issue of community

development. Ahmad and Miller state that the proclaimed values, objectives, and the methods associated with community development:

> ... have been used as a vehicle to satisfy a number of often quite contradictory purposes that span the political spectrum. (1997, p 270)

Perspectives of community development include those who view it as a mechanism for urban management, those who see it as a vehicle for radical social change and those who conservatively use it to promote individual and collective self-help in the face of declining state intervention. Ahmad and Miller (1997) argue that different opinions as to what constitutes community development hang together because of a common language based around notions such as empowerment, participation and inclusion. They also show that it is being brought out from the margins of service provision to centre stage, albeit with the strings of tight governmental control attached.

The complicated process of 'community' creation and development is made all the more so by the need for many in the formal regenerative agencies to project positive images of a place to the outside world. In these, aspects of 'community' are embellished and reconstructed in interesting ways.

## A typology of community initiatives

Not surprisingly, therefore, a great variety of community initiatives exist, and we found many different examples of them in the places we visited. Such differences make it difficult to group such initiatives and analytically categorise them. They vary in scale, scope, extent and form of community involvement, inherent philosophy and aspirations. The key that unlocks, and begins to make sense of, these differences is how community initiatives are started. Before examining cross-cutting issues that are common to most of them, however, we focus on the initiatives themselves, showing their differences and distinguishing features. To begin to make sense of these features, the community initiatives that we encountered in our research are divided into three groups. These broad groups are defined on the basis of how community projects are initiated, who is involved from the start and with which other community initiatives they are in conflict. Conflicts were the real eye-opener to divisions which separate one group of initiatives from another, all of which are tied up in the personalities of community project initiators (and coordinators) and their desperate fights against each other for funding. More is made of these conflicts later on in the report. The three categories of initiative are defined as:

- initiated by socially entrepreneurial immigrants;
- locally-initiated by committed local residents;
- formally-initiated by government and other organisations.

We would stress that this categorisation is in no sense intended to be definitive or universally applicable. Rather it is an heuristic device, limited in its scope to the community initiatives we investigated, but which nonetheless allows us tentatively to begin to group these initiatives into broad categories in terms of their processes of origin, development and conflicts. That said, we believe that it may be of more general value as a way of grouping such community initiatives. Our categorisation might also help avoid simplistic judgements as to their potential 'successes' and 'failures'.

## Initiated by socially entrepreneurial immigrants

This group is made up of projects set in motion by key individuals who have moved into a place and set up a community initiative. Socially entrepreneurial immigrants are often charismatic individuals, capturing the imagination of some of the existing residents of the local community, who are incorporated into the project as volunteers or paid workers.

Socially entrepreneurial immigrants who 'kick start' community initiatives often have good links, or are good at developing links, outside of the localities in which their projects are based. They are networked individuals with links with academic institutions, politicians, people within local government, key players within umbrella community development organisations, such as the Development Trust Association, other community organisations and, in one case that we came across, the royal family. This network of relationships outside a place helps to publicise their projects through media attention

when organising activities and being visited by famous people. As a result, these projects are often used as exemplary case studies in the literature of umbrella community development organisations. Their positive publicising helps them to transform outside perceptions of their place and to access funding.

The people that make up this group are often driven by particular agendas.

### Religion

A minister who moved onto the estate in 1986 has largely spearheaded the community initiatives of Penrhys Housing Estate. While he was born and brought up in Tylorstown, he left the Rhondda Valley, but subsequently came back to live on Penrhys. In 1989 he became the estate's minister and the Penrhys Partnership was formed in 1991. There are two arms to the Penrhys Partnership: the Partnership Ltd – a company limited by guarantee, and the Partnership Trust – a charity. Much of the community work on the estate is driven by his 'serving congregation' philosophy with an outlook on the person, the community and the world being about wholeness. Working on some of the initiatives are overseas volunteers and students, who are on placements, and through the community café, posters seek to educate their readers about world problems and how they can be helped through community work, such as the foods prepared and sold in the café. Llanfair, an independent member of the partnership, was opened in 1992, and forms the bedrock of the work on the estate, having a ripple effect on all the other initiatives. Llanfair was created from a derelict block of maisonettes gifted to Penrhys by Rhondda Borough Council and includes a chapel, café, nearly-new shop, crèche, minibus, education, music and art workrooms. The services and facilities are mostly run by unpaid volunteers.

Following the establishment of Llanfair, the Penrhys Partnership developed other initiatives including an amphitheatre, Y Ffynnon – a village centre facility and service complex (which houses a doctor's surgery, shops and offices along with residential accommodation), Cartref – a home for vulnerable residents and Canolfan Rhys – the arts and education centre. Reinforcing the communal ambience of Llanfair, with its volunteering ethic, Penrhys Partnership employees are expected to live as well as work on the estate.

### Radical, challenging institutional orthodoxies

The Arts Factory grew out of the Vale Community Business, an initiative that focused on landscaping and people with learning disabilities. A Mencap development worker, who changed jobs to work for Vale Community Business, spearheaded its transformation into The Arts Factory. Established in 1994, The Arts Factory moved to its current premises, rented from Rhondda Cynon Taff County Borough Council (RCTCBC), on Ferndale's Highfields Estate in 1995. The remit of the project has changed, seeking to embrace the community in its entirety, while building sustainable community enterprises, upskilling local people and providing high quality community facilities. At present, the initiative supports six community enterprises, each facilitated by a team of volunteers and trainees, with two employees – a team leader and a team trainer. The six enterprises are landscaping, public art, pottery, garden centre/plant nursery and two types of woodcraft. In December 1996 the initiative bought Trerhondda Chapel which is being renovated as a multi-use community resource.

A marketing manager with similar ideals joined The Arts Factory more recently and together the two spearhead and set the agenda for the initiative. Their offices are in windowless attics at the top of one of the buildings that house the enterprises, and in their offices, like everywhere else in the buildings, there are posters of influential activists, like Che Guevara, and daubed slogans on the walls. The project emphasises its commitment to decent pay for the 27 people it employs and the provision of 'useful work' (as opposed to 'useless toil') for the employees, volunteers and trainees alike. In total, the project has about 100 trainees and volunteers. Positive and direct in its approach, with a firm belief that asset ownership is the key to self-sustainability, it has had to endure difficult relationships with the local authority over issues such as the purchase of the chapel, which was destined for demolition. While relations with the local authority and local politicians have been problematic, relationships with key council officers have been good and this has been significant to the development of the project.

### Children- and young people-focused

Penygraig Community Project was initiated by a married couple, one with a background in youth and community work and originally from Scotland, the other in community arts and originally from Mountain Ash in the Cynon Valley. They met in Scotland, but returned to Wales in 1977 to work in the Rhondda's Penygraig. The project evolved from its original premises in the coal cellar of the probation service, funded by the Job Creation Programme and working with a local probation officer who promoted group work rather than working with individuals. In 1978, they were working with 80 young people, some of whom were on probation. The project moved to its present Cross Street site in 1980, renting the former offices of the local Industrial Cooperative Society from the local authority for a peppercorn rent. It also now works in a Baptist Chapel, which has been renovated into a flexible space – used as a play area and for performances, while the vestry is still used by a local congregation for its services.

The project has since expanded to work in the RCT area as a whole through its Community Access to Technology Project, Bridges Community Support Scheme and Outreach Play Scheme. The underlying philosophy of the project is grounded in youth work and encouraging child play and development for the child's sake and not only to support adults accessing work opportunities. The two directors emphasise that unlike the Labour government's emphasis on crèches and play schemes as a means of getting adults into employment, their work prioritises the needs of young people. They argue that working with young people is a good community development tool, attracting adult volunteers to the project, some of whom have been trained and employed as staff.

### Locally-initiated by committed local residents

The projects of this category are initiated by a group of local residents who seek to address the particular needs of a place – of *their* place – as they see them. A common theme inspiring all of these projects is first-hand experience of a place's tragic transformation since the closure of its pit(s) and the devastating repercussions of this for individuals, families and community life.

**Figure 7: Ollerton and Boughton Women's Centre**

Individuals are spurred into action to form groups for different reasons:

- Blaenllechau Community Regeneration came about through a creative writing group that was compiling and collecting information for a book, *Green, black and back*. The members of the group wanted to bring jobs, services and facilities back into the village.

- Ollerton and Boughton Women's Centre was initiated after an International Women's Day celebration at Ollerton's Dukeries Complex (see Figure 7). It was recognised by a group of local women that services and recreational and social space only serviced men and that women were facing increasing problems at home because of changes in their households related to unemployment.

- Ollerton and District Economic Forum emerged from the Mining Communities Support Group after unsuccessfully rallying to prevent the closure of Ollerton Colliery.

- Cynon Valley Credit Union was initiated by a group of Cynon Valley residents including miners from Tower Colliery who got together to invest their redundancy money into a successful employee buy-out bid to save the colliery.

While all of these initiatives are of some benefit to the wider place-based community, when they first started they often focused on a specific facility or issue. Once the project has developed and a service or facility has been established, then the initiative sometimes moves on to embrace wider community issues, even employing community development workers and other staff (although not always without problems). These projects can be categorised as falling into one of two types: originally facility-oriented or issue-oriented.

## Originally facility-oriented

In the case of some projects, the development of a community facility is the focus of attention. For instance, a group of residents in Maerdy started a local lottery to raise funds for the renovation of a former police station given to them for 80 years for an annual rent of £1. Over a period of four years they raised £48,000. Maerdy Community Centre is impressive and now houses a baby clinic, meeting and art rooms, a café, offices, and has been extended to include a theatre. A further extension is planned to accommodate an arts block. While a community development worker was employed to develop and expand the work of the project, the relationship between the worker and the executive committee proved problematic and so the worker was asked to leave. At present, the group of locals involved in the initiative continues to focus its attention on the renovated Police Station and the facilities that it contains. Other facility-oriented projects have found it similarly difficult to focus on community-wide issues, especially once a building has been developed and its revenue costs have to be met.

Projects such as Bryncynon Community Revival Strategy Ltd (BCRS) and Blaenllechau Community Regeneration have, however, had more success in community development work, establishing strong relationships between boards of directors (largely made up of community members) and project employees such as community development workers and project coordinators. Both of these projects generate income through renting out space for training and educational use, running income-generating enterprises and participating in the New Deal programme. Indeed, Bryncynon's receptionist is a voluntary sector New Deal trainee placement. Projects such as these also go on to develop and support community businesses. Blaenllechau Community Regeneration has two arms to it – a charitable trust and a trading arm (Blaenllechau Community Enterprise Ltd). Blaenllechau Community Enterprise Ltd now supports three local businesses – a crèche and café, both run from the centre, and a fish 'n' chips shop run from separate premises that the project owns. Community initiatives such as these are evolving all the time and developing new projects to access funding and income.

The above projects are, however, sometimes difficult to develop, precisely because of the strong connections of particular local residents with them. This is best shown in the case of Maerdy Community Centre, which is tightly constituted because of perceived fears that others might take control of the project for financial gain rather than for the sake of the project itself. To avoid this, the project has two forms of membership – ordinary and executive. Anyone can be an ordinary member. To be an executive member, an individual has to demonstrate a commitment to the project through volunteer work, making them eligible for executive membership, which is decided by the executive committee. The project currently has an ordinary membership of 60 people and 37 executive members. Only executive members can be voted onto the executive committee, which currently stands at 15. All this makes a closed and rule-bound organisation, but this is defended by the executive committee who have witnessed the demise of other local projects because of the deliberate exclusion of original initiators. Executive committee members claim that initiatives like that of Maerdy Community Centre involve considerable effort and time on the part of the locals involved and they do not want to see their hard work fail.

Issue-oriented

In contrast to projects that develop out of the establishment of a community (resource) centre, other locally-initiated projects are a response to a particular expressed or perceived need. These initiatives benefit local people through the delivery of a particular service and/or by creating jobs but are not informed by concepts of all-embracing community development. These locally initiated projects include Valleys Childcare Ltd, Valleys Furniture Recycling and Cynon Valley Credit Union. These initiatives provide, respectively, the following services:

- childcare and crèche provision in places such as Fernhill Estate to relieve mothers to be able to seek advice, support and access training opportunities;
- cheap furniture provision for those on benefits;
- access to low interest loans on the basis of ability to save rather than ownership of collateral, regardless of previous financial standing.

There is in addition some potential for such issue-oriented projects to become self-sustaining community businesses. Valleys Childcare Ltd has secured contracts with Aberdare College, RCT Community Education, Mountain Ash Comprehensive School, Save the Children Fund and National Children's Homes and is looking for more contracts. Valleys Furniture Recycling (VFR) is looking to generate income through developing training outputs and at present VFR employs a trainer who is supervising two trainees. Not only does their training generate a £200 weekly income for the project, but their work on mending and upholstering furniture adds value and creates goods that can be sold at higher prices. However, these enterprises operate in deprived places where many people are unable to afford the full costs of services and goods. Also, they encourage and train unemployed volunteers and, in the case of VFR, work with people who lack confidence, but find training courses that aim to increase employability impossible to afford at first. While these enterprises aim to develop income generating strands, because of their objectives, they will always be reliant on funding.

## Formally-initiated by government and other organisations

The projects that make up this group are initiated and controlled by the formal sector, particularly local authorities. Consequently, local people's reaction to them is, sometimes, at best one of indifference, at worst one of confrontation and opposition.

A good – or bad – example of the latter is the project on Perthcelyn. Here, having successfully secured funding to build a new school and address the estate's problems, the local authority-led strategy began work on the estate. However, this failed to meet the needs of the local community as local people perceived them. At this point the Residents' and Tenants' Association (RTA) pulled out of the project and established its own busy base further along the road from that of the shuttered offices of the strategy (Figure 8). The RTA's reasons for leaving the strategy are a frustration resulting from its aims and needs being over-ridden by the aims and actions of the local authority. The RTA accuses the local authority of not adequately responding to the estate's needs, relating to problems of crime, drugs and speeding cars, highlighted in a survey of the estate. CCTV cameras are focused on local authority-owned property and not in places where local residents want them to be, newly-laid roads are sinking and fencing has replaced dry stone walls with gardens collapsing through gaps onto pavements and large gaps between the bottom of the fence and the ground allowing animals and children to escape from gardens (Figure 9). For the RTA, such issues exemplify the inadequate response of the local authority to the needs of the community. Problems highlighted in the survey continue to persist, with residents living in fear of one or two key individuals on the estate involved in crime and drug dealing. Petty crime persists, with witnesses who take action against criminals often victimised and living in fear.

Other initiatives experiencing similar problems include the Tichfield Ward Regeneration project. Here, Mansfield Diamond Partnership bid for and secured £3.8 million of SRB funding to complete a £9 million programme of regeneration for the

ward (which includes the town centre). Crime and community safety are identified as particular areas of concern and over £140,000 has been ring-fenced for projects to tackle these issues. An early meeting between Mansfield Diamond Partnership (which is made up of representatives from Mansfield District Council, Nottinghamshire County Council, North Nottinghamshire Training and Enterprise Council, Mansfield 2010 and Mansfield CVS) and local residents, demonstrated significant discrepancies between the aims of the partnership and the demands of the residents. For Mansfield Diamond Partnership the aim of the meeting was to give local residents the opportunity to decide the best ways of involving local people in the regeneration process. On the other hand, local residents only wanted to list the needs of the Tichfield ward – one of the most disaffected and deprived in Mansfield. Since the meeting, the process of community consultation has included youth consultation, interviews, as well as a postal survey to all Tichfield households (although at the time of writing the results of this consultation exercise were yet to emerge).

Dulais Valley Partnership is another initiative that has experienced problems engaging with local residents in its projects. The initiative is different from the others that are considered in this research in that its remit includes the regeneration of not one village or community but an entire valley. The Partnership works from a building gifted to them by British Telecom in Seven Sisters, where its four employees (funded by RECHAR 2) are based. Neath Port Talbot CBC (NPTCBC) put together the RECHAR bid after surveying the residents of the valley. The initiative has no membership, which means that the Board of the Dulais Valley Partnership is difficult to remove. In addition to having a strong presence on the board, NPTCBC coordinates the initiative's finances. Although the initiative started in April 1997, its main success to date is establishing a job opportunities information point at the Partnership's office in Seven Sisters, developing a link with Swansea's Jobcentre to access details of job vacancies and matching them to jobs wanted by some Dulais Valley Residents. Other projects are also beginning to materialise with a community minibus purchased in December 1999 and the launch of an out-of-school club, which will provide quality, affordable childcare for children aged 4-12 years. Some projects are proving more difficult to pursue, such as the conversion of the disused Cwmdulais Centre into a multi-use community centre. There are also problems with the development of community businesses, such as the Welsh Hardwood Industry, for which the Partnership, at the time of the research, was pessimistically awaiting the results of a feasibility study and market research on its potential customer base.

While this group contains the most problematic community initiatives, given the difficulties involved in rallying and maintaining local support in places that have lost heart, there are also examples of projects that have been more successful. The Mansfield Woodhouse Community Development Group (MWCDG) has successfully worked with Mansfield District Council to renovate the Park Road Resource Centre, a multi-use facility that includes a cyber-café. MWCDG was established as the Regeneration Agency, an unincorporated association, and run by a management

**Figure 8: Shuttered offices on the Perthcelyn Community Strategy**

**Figure 9: Perthcelyn Estate**

committee made up of local people, along with representatives of Nottinghamshire County Council and Mansfield District Council. While the project has had its problems, with a few locals leaving the group, local commitment is still good and the project is enthusiastically led by the chairperson, a local resident.

Penywaun Enterprise Partnership has similarly had some success, renovating a 19th-century chapel to become a training and enterprise centre called the Cana Centre (Figure 10). The project was spearheaded by Cynon Valley Council, and the particular efforts of a council officer, now the project manager. This person became involved initially via a major consultative exercise after a horrific murder on Penywaun Estate, which resulted in bad publicity for the place. Penywaun Enterprise Partnership is answerable to its membership, made up of local residents, local organisations and groups and outside organisations and individuals with a role in Penywaun and Trenant Estates. While the energies of MWCDG have had to focus on the facility because of worries about funding, Penywaun Enterprise Partnership has had better success in relation to wider issues of community development, although it also has to fight to access adequate funding to maintain the building and continue the initiative.

## Wider initiatives

The development of these effective partnership workings in South Wales relates in part to the length of time that the people have had to adjust to, and cope with, the problems created by colliery closures. For many people on the coalfields, the idea that employment in the mines was a thing of the past proved difficult and painful to grasp. The disbelief and sense of injustice unsettled them. Many people talked to us of the mine closing in terms normally reserved for the death of a close friend or family member. In South Wales the people had had longer to grieve and adjust. As such there seemed a considerable awareness of the need to work strategically with ideas of partnership. We were pointed to a number of schemes that were seen to be successful within RCT and in the adjoining valleys.

One of these, the Dulais Valley Partnership, we have already mentioned. We spent some time visiting and talking with its active members in and around Severn Sisters. This partnership provides an example of an initiative extending beyond the level of one village or locality to embrace a wider area and community. In our initial classification of community initiatives,

**Figure 10: The Cana Centre on the Penywaun Estate**

projects that attempt a wider perspective are usually formally initiated or developed by socially entrepreneurial immigrants. They laso focus on one specific issue. Dulais Valley Partnership is unusual because it embraces multiple issues in its holistic approach to regeneration involving issues of tourism, inward investment, education, training and leisure activities.

The other wider area initiatives we encountered tended to be issue specific. For example, the issue of lifelong learning drives the Valleys Initiative for Adult Education (VIAE), which aims "to widen participation in education and training for non-traditional learners in South Wales Valleys communities so as to assist community economic regeneration" (VIAE, 1999, p 1). VIAE operates from an office in Ebbw Vale and has helped to coordinate a network of pan-Valleys horizontal partnerships that linked across local authority areas. Concerned with developing policy in the area of adult education it was also involved in several vertical partnerships that involved policy makers and practitioners as well as adult learners.

The activities of two other initiatives with a wide geographical spread – Valley and Vale and RCT Community Arts – revolved around community arts. These initiatives have a strong history of working with a range of different individuals and communities, enabling individuals and groups to express themselves – their opinions, ideas, frustrations – through a range of different media and activities. Their work occasionally has some unexpected consequences. People working together on a community arts project can find that this experience of creative cooperation leads them to think about and question other aspects of their lives and local environment. Occasionally it can galvanise groups of people into setting up their own community regeneration initiatives. It was RCT Community Arts that played an important part in the formation of the Blaenllechau Community Regeneration initiative through its work with the creative writing group mentioned earlier.

A few initiatives that started with a focus on a particular community are attempting to broaden their remits. This is best exemplified by the Penygraig Community Project which established a Bridges Community Support Scheme in April 1996 with funding from the NLCB. With over 20

years' experience of innovative community development work which began in Penygraig, a skilled team continues to use this approach, spearheaded by the two directors, to support other communities. After a period of research and consultation with local people and agencies to identify areas of most need, they now play a key role in the regeneration work of Penyrenglyn and Rhydyfelin, and run outreach activities in numerous valleys communities. Issues that affect young people continue to play an important part in their work. This was made clear in April 1999 when Penygraig Community Project changed its name to Valley Kids.

Clearly, there are good reasons for the remits of initiatives to embrace broad areas rather than specific places – particularly in areas like the South Wales Valleys that are made up of places with similar problems. How this is achieved is another matter – especially for initiatives that take an holistic approach to regeneration and are not only focused on a particular issue. As we have shown, problems may emerge when a local authority spearheads a wider area-based approach. Problems may also arise when local community initiatives widen their areas of influence, with host community groups occasionally resentful of their presence – perceiving them to have accessed funds for which they should have bid and over which they should have control. These ongoing conflicts and disputes over resources are intimately tied up with questions of deprivation and legitimacy. They are persistent features of these new community initiatives.

As such, these examples of 'failure' and 'success' raise broader questions about the appropriate role(s) of socially entrepreneurial immigrants, local authorities, and a host of other organisations involved in various ways in regeneration initiatives. They also raise questions as to what would constitute an appropriate politics of regeneration and (re)development. There is certainly abundant evidence of imagination and enthusiasm, although this in itself does not automatically guarantee the 'success' of a given project. Beyond, this, however, there lies the critical issue of how to sustain local enthusiasm and imagination in the face of what is often seen as bureaucratic indifference, a constant battle to secure funding, and the resultant threat – or reality – of the collapse of projects.

# 5

# Issues of community development

## Introduction

Community development is very often driven by the agendas of those who initiate it. Its form varies according to this. The precise reasons why people start up projects differ, but they are always bounded by the specificities of their locality, its physical characteristics, history and people. Community projects are shaped by their context, making their successes – or failures – particular to a place and the people who live there.

## The place of community initiatives

Community initiatives in Mansfield and RCT are located in deprived places (see Tables 5 and 6). These are places with significant levels of petty crime, and derelict and polluted environments. Here the population has been growing more slowly than the national average. Some of the most enterprising people, or at least a substantial number of those of working age, have left. As we have seen, many who remain are disillusioned and depressed, as are their local economies. Reducing public sector involvement in these places has accelerated the erosion of their service and facility provision. Public transport is inadequate and unreliable. Quality of housing is poor, childcare provision is inadequate and healthcare is not of the best, with places like these having problems recruiting general practitioners. Owners of homes that have depreciated in market value are locked into places with few, and largely only low quality and poorly paid, jobs. Those who attempt to seek employment elsewhere and commute to work are regularly hampered by 'postcode prejudice', an experience that they share with people living in 'the wrong part' of large cities.

All of this has a downward and cumulative spiralling impact on former coalfield places, reinforcing high levels of economic inactivity, which further feeds existing socioeconomic problems.

Given the marginality of these places in relation to the private and public sectors, the community sector has to work in the empty spaces that remain. Empty because of the lack of service and facility provision, inadequate private sector investment and little, if any, indigenous growth of SMEs. All of this is set against past dependencies on a single industry which has, for the most part, closed, followed by initiatives that focused on inadequate training leading to little in the way of job opportunities. This is the context within which the 'third sector' operates: people who are demoralised and lack confidence in places that accentuate feelings of marginality and isolation in their relation to the 'outside' world. In these circumstances 'success' is measured on a very small scale indeed. Seemingly tiny successes can have great significance.

## Sustaining community initiatives: how?

*In pursuit of an illusion: the Holy Grail of self-sustainability*

Most projects aspire to self-sustainability, especially when bidding for funding. In reality, however, many see achieving self-sustainability as an impossible dream. Some community initiatives emphasise the contradiction of self-sustainability and community development, with community development being an impossible objective without the support of external funding and self-sustainability only becoming possible once a community has been adequately developed. Even some projects with community businesses view such funding as a necessity. This is because community businesses operate in places in which people are unable to pay the full cost of provision of their services and private business is unlikely to set up because of a lack of market and the risk of – at best – poor profit margins or – at worst – losses. Also, they have to compete with other 'businesses' that hover in a grey zone around the boundary between illegal and legal economies, periodically slipping from one side of the boundary to the other.

One long-established community initiative has set its face against community businesses as a means to create income in pursuit of financial self-sustainability. The people there argued that supporting and managing such businesses required a different expertise, skills and knowledge to those needed for community development. For them, business objectives meant compromising those of community development. In their view, a concern with increased profit margins would override those of community development. They understood that community businesses could potentially lead to the self-sustainability of initiatives and in this way bring benefit to the locality. Nevertheless, they believed that prioritising income generation could only lead to too little emphasis being placed on the public sector savings generated by the community sector. Despite the difficulties of precisely quantifying such savings, some community initiatives argue that their public sector savings out-weigh their costs to the public sector. This was best exemplified by a project based in Penyrenglyn (in the Rhondda Fawr Valley), on the Mount Libanus Estate. As well as working on community-wide issues, it also works closely with individuals. For example, some four years ago the project worked with a woman with serious learning difficulties, who had three children, two of whom were in care. The project provided her with one-to-one tuition and support and encouraged her to attend courses at the centre on basic living. No longer so dependent on public sector resources, she has kept her third child and is now more accepted on the estate with her boy being invited to local children's parties – an example of what can be achieved in enhancing individual's lives and community cohesion.

Only three of the projects examined in this research viewed economic self-sustainability to be a realistic possibility. Even for them, however, this is a qualified acceptance and comes with stipulations, central to which is the endowment of assets ("and not liabilities"). Others are sceptical because the ownership of a considerable amount of assets is needed before the revenue costs of a community enterprise can be fully supported. Also, they argue that the work of such community enterprises involves the employment and volunteering of the long-term unemployed and most 'unemployable'. A consequence of this is to create a far from level playing field when tendering for contracts because of the extra length of time that work takes and the additional costs that this involves.

## Public sector funding: enabling or constraining?

At present, all the community initiatives considered in this research are dependent on public sector funding. This raises considerable doubts as to the extent to which they can be thought of as constituting part of a 'third sector' – independent of both market and state. Moreover, the structures of public funding affect the objectives and characteristics of community initiatives, sometimes for the worse, with the development of projects often being constrained by funding stipulations, monitoring requirements and performance criteria. In our discussions, the issue of funding and the problems associated with it (the ever present need for form filling and accountability) predominated. There is some evidence that the government has also become more aware of the consistent list of complaints and difficulties identified by these local activists. We list a few of them.

### Time consuming

Key actors for all the projects emphasised the amount of time dedicated to accessing funding, which reduced the time available for community development work. This is exemplified in Bryncynon Community Revival Strategy Ltd's business plan, which states unequivocally that the "constant pursuit of grant aid diverts expertise, energy and resources away from meeting the needs of the community" (BCRS, 1998, p 12). This is but one of many examples.

## Complexity

Project managers for community initiatives find devising and completing applications for funding to be a complicated process that takes too much time and effort. Successful community initiatives often, of necessity, draw upon a variety of sources of funds at any one time, all of which require reports that cover and emphasise different issues and relate to different reporting periods.

## Demands for data

The following demands of funding bodies are often problematic for community initiatives.

- **Quantifiable outputs:** Funding bodies typically require information demonstrating the quantifiable outputs of community initiatives, central to which is the number of jobs created. Not only can this be difficult to quantify with any degree of meaningful precision but an overemphasis on such quantifiable outputs can also mean that other important information about the work of such projects remains hidden. Sometimes just engaging with people in a place is a big task, never mind getting them into employment. The extent to which the work of a project is effective for the people it is meant to be helping is difficult to quantify, whether it be transforming a house into a home with subsidised furniture or providing a meeting point for women over 40 where they can drink coffee and "have a laugh". These effects of projects may remain invisible precisely because of their successes being impossible to quantify. As such, they are being ignored and undervalued.
- **New projects:** Many of the community initiatives considered in this research stated that funders sought new projects and not the financing of existing projects to allow initiatives to consolidate their work. Instead of strengthening their existing and successful initiatives, project managers and workers are expected to regularly develop new ideas for projects to access funding.
- **Short-termism:** A common cause for concern is the length of time for which funding bodies finance projects. Three years and less of funding is considered an inadequate length of time for community initiatives to develop substantially and meet their objectives. Short-term funding causes

insecurities, which prevents community initiatives from fully realising their potential.
- **Match funding:** Often applications for public sector funding need to demonstrate that match funding is available from other sources. The problems of accessing matching funding are a concern, with some community initiatives fearing that only larger bodies with their own funding sources are able to draw down funding from elsewhere.
- **Capital or revenue?** One community initiative highlighted the issue that funding bodies, such as the NLCB, fund either capital *or* revenue costs but rarely both. This means, for example, that smaller community initiatives have to somehow absorb revenue costs once they have built a facility.

## Lack of feedback

There is a general concern that funding bodies and organisations such as the Wales European Programme Executive do not provide enough feedback or support to community initiatives when they bid for funding. Only rarely do potential funders and gate-keepers to funding visit community initiatives and discuss their bids, objectives and project plans. When bids are unsuccessful it is also often difficult for community initiatives to obtain useful information which explains why they failed to get funding.

## Competition

Funding structures cause competition between community initiatives as they attempt to access the same finite sources of finance. Within given areas, such competition leads to clashes between initiatives, particularly those started by socially entrepreneurial immigrants and those that are initiated by local residents. Locally-initiated projects often feel that they are working in the shadows of well-publicised and high-profile projects directed by socially entrepreneurial immigrants, and have difficulties in competing with them for funding. Furthermore, funding-related arguments occur because of accusations that locally-initiated projects' facilities are included (not always with their agreement or knowledge) in the successful bids of socially entrepreneurial immigrants. Locally-initiated projects argue that they do not themselves financially benefit from such inclusion and are then unable to apply for their own funding because of duplication within the same postcode area. Socially entrepreneurial immigrants counter that locally-initiated projects benefit from their support and advice when setting up and that they do benefit from inclusion in their successful bids, for example, as the recipients of outreach services and other projects. These arguments often descend to bickering and are deeply counter-productive. They demonstrate a basic problem: there is too great a competition for limited sources of funding. In many areas of life competition may be seen as a positive factor encouraging innovation and change. Not so in these places. Here the rules of competition limit cooperation between parties who would benefit from solidarity. What is lost is the cohesion of these community initiatives.

### Private sector investment: on the fringes of the market economy

Our research indicated that the private sector has contributed little in the way of direct financial investment to the development of community initiatives. We did find examples where companies had donated goods and services to local community initiatives. Examples of this type of support include:

- RJ Budge donated two portacabins to Ollerton and Boughton Women's Centre;
- local shops in Ollerton donate prizes to Ollerton and Boughton Girls' Project;
- Royal Mail donated a van to VFR and Cook and Arkwright provided a free building survey.

These donations, while welcomed by the people concerned, are pitifully small in the general context of economic need and provision. In this way, the coalfield areas face problems similar to many rural areas where few large local employers exist with the capacity to provide ongoing and sustaining support. However, the coalfields do have an extensive industrial past and one which has historically generated large resources. The miners' pension fund is one example. It is possible that this could be used to the advantages of some of the most deprived areas. In 1999, the Coalfield Regeneration Trust urged companies that had benefited from the investment of colliers' pension funds to develop funds and form partnerships to work on the

economic regeneration of the coalfields (see *The Guardian* 26 October 1999).

## Servicing community initiatives: types of community initiatives

Almost all the community initiatives studied in this research provide services rather than produce goods. There are many reasons why manufacturing-related enterprises are under-represented in the community sector. Often individualistic in their origins, developing one individual's innovative ideas, they do not touch the community in the same way that service provision might. More generally, successful manufacturing enterprises require higher levels of capital outlay. Service provision in contrast is often labour-intensive, providing readily visible evidence of the work of the enterprise. It also requires less finance to initiate (Pearce, 1993). The one project we examined which produced goods was The Arts Factory in South Wales. Some of the goods produced by the initiative – plants, pottery and woodcrafts – were sold through its plant nursery, which occupied one part of the project's premises. However, The Arts Factory's production facilities involved relatively low start-up costs and production there is labour intensive. In addition to its manufacturing side it provides training and will soon offer other services (small cinema, activities for young people and so on) through (its soon to be completed) converted chapel. The services on offer in the groups that we examined include:

- the provision of subsidised furniture for those on benefits;
- saving and loans opportunities;
- out-of-school activities for young people;
- drop-in facilities and counselling;
- crèches and childcare provision;
- courses and training;
- transport provision;
- music, arts and theatre-based services;
- landscaping services;
- café and catering provision.

In areas in which a number of projects were operating, there was sometimes a tendency to duplicate service provision. This was particularly the case for courses and training, café and childcare provision. This could be a problem, producing a serial monotony of service provision and locally-based service providers competing with one another and with neighbouring places for users. However, the cultural characteristics of places and the pride that local people take in 'their place' often generates a demand for each place to have its own service provision.

Localities define themselves in relation to one another and where this process is intense it can lead to strong community identities and with it the demand for their own service providers. This is reinforced, especially in the case of the South Wales Valleys, by the physical characteristics of places and the difficulties and expense involved in accessing service providers in neighbouring places. Former coalfield communities contain a significant proportion of people on sickness-related benefits and disaffected people who have been unemployed for a lengthy period of time, limiting both their ability to travel and their confidence in approaching service providers outside their own communities. Until such issues of unemployment, poverty and lack of transport, and the problems that they in turn engender, are eased, then individual communities will continue to need their own service provision. A corollary of the poverty and lack of confidence that is rife in such marginalised and deprived places is that service providers working in them will need continued public sector funding because of difficulties in operating as businesses in places where people are unable to afford their services. Consequently, successful community development work is needed before such businesses are a realistic possibility.

## Effective community initiatives?

At the very least, community initiatives effect the conversion of derelict or disused buildings into (mostly) useful facilities. Examples of these include the disused cooperative in Warsop Vale which is being converted into a community resource centre and the chapel on Penywaun Estate that has been converted into the Cana Centre – a community training facility. Conversions are mostly successful, transforming eyesores into community assets, but occasionally projects run into difficulties with high revenue costs and poor renovation work. For example, the Penrhiwceiber Hall committee, from which the Penrhiwceiber Community Revival Strategy Group rents space, is unhappy with the hall's conversion – while the exterior looks good (Figure 11), internal features hamper the community's use of the facility. The renovation of the building began in 1993 after Cynon Valley Borough Council successfully bid for £300,000 of

**Figure 11: Penrhiwceiber Hall**

Welsh Office funding. According to community members, the funding was misspent by employing firms from outside the area. The work of these companies resulted in a poor and inadequate renovation of the building. Community members have a long list of complaints. As they see them, the building's problems include:

- doors which are now too small to allow stage scenery to pass through them;
- the floor is not level;
- there is no access for disabled people;
- the lighting is unsatisfactory;
- the stage which was previously movable is now immovable;
- fixed chairs prevent the multi-use of space.

A few of the firms involved in the renovation work went bankrupt, so that some of the work and goods that had been paid for never materialised. While Boughton Pumping Station in Nottinghamshire has been beautifully converted, a combination of high start-up costs and capital costs only being covered by funding sources has forced the initiative temporarily to prioritise income generating schemes. However, 'Pumping life back into the coalfield community' is the enterprise's mission statement (see Figure 12) and it continues to work towards this through employing and training local people, organising family fun-days and providing a facility that locals can use for such events as wedding receptions and end-of-term college parties.

Meeting revenue costs is a concern for other initiatives but, for the most part, in addition to making physical improvements to places, they provide accessible facilities for local communities. In addition to benefiting the users of their facilities and services, community initiatives help those who play a role in the daily running and management of service and facility provision and goods production. The Regeneration Alliance is a group of six (Bryncynon, Penywaun, The Arts Factory, Penygraig, Penyrenglyn, Blaenllechau [Rhondda Housing Association – associate member of the Development Trust Association]) community initiatives based in the Cynon and Rhondda Valleys, all of which share common concerns and objectives supported by their membership of the Development Trust Association. Between them they employ over 120 people, making the

**Figure 12: Boughton Pumping Station's mission statement**

community sector a significant employer in the area. The number of volunteers and trainees with whom they work is even greater, further extending the scope of the projects' influence.

Many of these employees are locals, the majority of them are also female. This is similarly the case for volunteering, although volunteers for the Boughton-based Furniture Project and VFR are mostly male. Often volunteers move on into employment. For example, VFR assisted 42% of its volunteers to secure paid work in 1997. Community initiatives emphasise, however, that volunteering is not just about training and assisting people into employment. At a meeting with a consultancy company employed by RCTCBC to research the needs and objectives of the community sector in relation to EU Objective 1 funding, a representative of The Arts Factory emphasised that community development work meant more than job creation and preparing people for work. It also teaches people how to feel involved, how to be a part of a team, how to become part of the community. These sentiments are put into action by The Arts Factory, which values the contributions of volunteers and employees equally, creating a positive atmosphere in the place and plenty of 'banter' among the different teams of workers. Other projects had similar positive atmospheres, best exemplified by Ollerton and Boughton Women's Centre, Blaenllechau's BELL Centre, Bryncynon's Development Centre, the Boughton-based Furniture Project and VFR.

While the above demonstrates the mostly positive effects of community initiatives on places, this study did identify instances in which it seemed that the beneficial effects to the community were more ambivilent. Such instances only occasionally occurred within the category of community projects that were formally initiated, in which the principal beneficiaries seemed to be those employed by the project to facilitate community development. This highlightes the problematic nature of the term 'community' in such circumstances. Given the inherent heterogeneity of people in places, community empowerment sometimes involves only a few individuals rather than a larger collective. As such, it can involve processes of social exclusion as well as of inclusion. In exceptional circumstances, it seems as if only very few individuals directly involved in these projects benefit from them – and in these circumstances the concept of 'community empowerment'; becomes particularly problematic.

# 6

# The right context ... for community development?

## Introduction

There are a number of issues that militate against the creation of a supportive context for community development within coalfield places. In particular there are continuing difficulties as a result of financial constraints and the complications posed by a stifling and confusing web of different policies – none of which endow communities with any meaningful power to spearhead the regeneration of their places.

## The financial context

According to the Coalfields Task Force report (1998), the coalfields fall below national and regional averages in their uptake of National Lottery funds. Furthermore, they have missed out on funding opportunities because of criteria used in relation to the Index of Local Conditions (and the Index of Local Deprivation) and the use of Standard Spending Assessments to allocate funding to coalfield local authorities has worked against them. These issues are currently being addressed by the government and other bodies such as the NLCB so that coalfields can increase their shares of these funding streams. What is currently lacking, however – and it is an absence that is likely to remain despite such changes – is a secure financial context for the regeneration of coalfield places.

There is little, if any, new money being specifically pumped into the regeneration of coalfields. In its response to the Coalfields Task Force, the government announced an additional £354 million for coalfields over the next three years (see Table 4). Most of this is not new money, however. Moreover, it is less than the

sum that has been generated from the pensions of former British Coal employees and which has accrued to the Treasury. The Coalfields Task Force identifies the two schemes for former British Coal employees – the Mineworkers' Pension Scheme (MPS) and the British Coal Staff Superannuation Scheme (BCSSS) and states that:

> At the time of the privatisation of the coal industry, it was agreed that the Department of Trade and Industry (DTI) would act as guarantor in the event of any deficit in the funds and would benefit from 50% of any surpluses generated. The investments have performed very well in recent years, and formal actuarial valuations have declared surpluses in the two funds totalling £2 billion. As a result, the DTI stands to receive payments of £150m a year over a 10-year period. A further BCSSS surplus has recently been announced, resulting in a new 10-year stream of payments to the DTI of over £60m a year. We understand that additional substantial surpluses are expected from MPS at the time of the next valuation. (CTF, 1998, para 6.39)

These windfall gains from the pension schemes have, as required by the 1994 Coal Industry Act, been paid into the Treasury's Consolidated Fund. In recognition of, and in response to, this the government stated that it would endow £10 million of additional resources to the Coalfields Regeneration Trust. But this does no more than return a small fraction of these funds generated on the coalfields by former coalminers to coalfield places.

Rather than prioritising the redistribution of finance to help reduce inequalities in standards of living, the government is, above all, committed to streamlining programmes of policy implementation to prevent duplication, overlap and the waste of resources. This thinking is at the heart of proposals for the government's new RDAs, which are to coordinate and include the regional regeneration work of English Partnerships and the Rural Development Commission and the administration of the SRB without any new sources of finance. RDAs, then, are charged to construct coherent frameworks for regional regeneration without the introduction of significant additional resources or a new stream of funding.

In recent years the largest source of funding for coalfield areas has been the EU. Although the precise amount channelled into the coalfields is difficult to quantify because their boundaries and those of wider EU assisted areas do not coincide, it has been estimated that English coalfields receive £200 million a year in EU regional aid (CTF, 1998, para 6.5). Match funding from local contributions enhances the impact of this aid. Much of this aid to coalfield areas comes via Objective 2 support for industrial areas, although South Yorkshire and the South Wales Valleys have now been made eligible for the top-priority funding allocated to Objective 1. If we add Merseyside, which includes parts of the Lancashire coalfield, it becomes clear that the British coal districts rank among the most deprived areas of the EU. Another significant aspect of EU support is its RECHAR programme which has been worth around £25 million a year to coalfield areas in England and all coalfields (in addition to the rest of the UK) benefit from European Social Fund support for training and retraining under Objectives 3 and 4.

With the EU's present framework for allocating funding ending in December 1999, new structures come into play in 2000 which will have direct and problematic consequences for the UK's coalfields. Problems will arise because the new EU funding framework includes the demise of the RECHAR programme and the restructuring of Objective 1 and Objective 2 funding. For the period 2000-06, EU aid will be targeted on the neediest of places, with those allocated Objective 1 status receiving 69.7% of EU structural funds and those defined as Objective 2 status, a much smaller 11.5%. The

criteria used to determine the status of a place is a further source of difficulty, with Objective 1 areas needing to fall below 75% of the EU average for GDP per head and Objective 2 areas needing to have above EU average unemployment. On the basis of the geographical units used by the EU to determine levels of funding, South Yorkshire, West Wales and the Valleys, Cornwall and the Isles of Scilly will join Merseyside in receiving Objective 1 status (Local Government International Bureau, 1999, p 53). While three of the Objective 1 areas have historical roots in coalmining, other former coalfields have failed to secure this allocation. Additionally, in light of the partial nature of unemployment statistics, the Coalfields Task Force report shows that many coalfield areas fail to qualify for Objective 2 status. It is worth noting that as the EU extends further eastwards into Europe the average level of GDP per head will fall and average unemployment rates will rise. This takes on added significance since in the future the UK government's own assisted areas (Development Areas and Intermediate Areas) are "likely to be tied more closely to the EU map of Objective 1 and 2 regions" (CTF, 1998, para 6.22). This means that those coalfield areas falling through the gaps of EU criteria for structural funds will lose out again in relation to other places in terms of their eligibility for firms located within them to receive Regional Selective Assistance.

## Governing communities: partnerships and the impacts of a complex policy environment

An emphasis on economic development is central to governmental 'joined-up thinking' as the route to achieving sustainable growth. For the government, the key to the regeneration of deprived places lies in their integration into the formal economy through economic development policies. This will involve realising the job creating potential of both FDI and indigenous SME growth via the provision of an adequately trained workforce so that local labour supply matches their labour demands. While social and physical regeneration supports economic development, and vice versa, economic development is seen as the key.

The New Labour government has unleashed a series of agendas and policies on the UK that are intended to impact positively on deprived places and to facilitate sustainable growth. The result of these though is a complicated context of programmes, targeted at a tangled mosaic of partially overlapping areas, spearheaded by different departments. Set against such a context, the former coalfields are affected by the government's workfare schemes and focus on coalfields and particularly deprived places through, respectively, its Coalfields Task Force and Social Exclusion Unit. The coalfields also have to stay aware of the government's area initiatives based around the notion of zones for joined-up solutions to problems of health and employment. While the government is attempting to devise cross-cutting solutions, bringing together departments to tackle the identified needs of particular places through, for example, the New Deal for Communities, so far, this has only added to the confusing context of programmes within which the community sector must work.

An important part of the government's agenda is partnership working. As outlined earlier, many partnerships are driven by the funding criteria, which stipulate their existence as a necessary condition of bidding for funding. As a result, setting up partnerships to bid for funding does not necessarily promote cooperation, but rather funding structures encourage competition between and within places for limited resources. Partnerships, then, are often termed 'marriages of convenience' with agencies and organisations 'getting into bed together'. Not all such arranged marriages are monogamous, however. Occasionally agencies are added to partnerships without any consultation, for funding reasons, in a sort of involuntary and enforced polygamy. Not only is the context complex, but it is also competitive and as such encourages instrumental and cynical behaviour.

For the government the inclusion of all organisations and agencies representing a place is seen as crucial to partnership working. The inclusion of organisations and individuals that represent people who live in a place is seen as especially important. The government promotes the inclusion of local interests in partnerships because "action must be tailored to local circumstances and take account of local needs" (DETR, 1997, p 7). Rarely, however, do partners

possess equal amounts of power. For example, the Welsh Development Agency firmly put itself at the centre of partnership working when drawing up its partnership structure for the Cynon Valley. A representative of English Partnerships demonstrated the existence of asymmetries in power in pointing out – light-heartedly but revealingly – that other agencies and organisations have to work with English Partnerships "'cos we have got the money!" Those with direct access to funding sources wield the greatest amount of power in and on partnerships, leaving representatives of the community sector on their periphery. Frequently, community representation on partnerships plays little more than a role of strategy implementation rather than helping to formulate regeneration agendas. On occasion, their inclusion seemed clearly to be little more than token representation to ensure that a tick could be placed in the relevant box on an application for funding.

Not only does access to resources empower some partners more than others but so too does association with larger areas, the representatives of which disparagingly accuse those operating within smaller geographical units as parochial and lacking a 'wider vision'. This was especially the case for Mansfield where there is a two-tiered local government structure with both District and County Councils contributing to partnerships. While organisations and agencies in such circumstances come together to access funds and negotiate a coherent strategy and framework of action, each has its own agenda, affected by different pressures and responsibilities. Somehow, however, those who live in a place or represent smaller geographical units are less influential because of their supposedly more limited strategic vision. The problem for local partners is that their agendas are often more transparent than those of other partners and are unashamedly focused on local issues and this works against them:

> "Because members were so parochial and had their own 'pet' schemes, they never thought on a cooperative basis, about the needs of the whole community...." (Social Services, Durham County Council)

Too often, then, local involvement and community representation on partnerships is not to do with empowerment but with the devolution of responsibility to the community sector to bring about the regeneration of local communities and economies. Power is still held at the apex of spatial and political hierarchies, even at the level of RDAs that are to respond to government agendas rather than to regional and local needs. Sometimes it seems that 'community empowerment' is more about blaming communities for their failures rather than assisting them to tackle constructively their problems as they see them in ways that they devise.

Finally, the aims and aspirations of the community sector sometimes do not coincide with those of the public sector. For example, a meeting between RCTCBC and representatives of community initiatives in RCT to discuss the strategy for Objective 1 funding revealed that the two work very differently. The community sector, especially socially entrepreneurial immigrants, is more prone to experimental approaches and risk taking while the public sector adheres to a more conservative and cautious approach. The two sides talk different languages and think differently about how best to tackle the problems facing them. More generally, various organisations and agencies have different visions for the community sector, different ideas as to what its aims and purposes ought to be. Formal sector organisations work within the central government's agenda for sustainable regeneration, the key to which is seen to be economic development within the context defined by a market economy, and a resultant continuing reliance on quantifiable outputs related to getting people into jobs and 'making work pay'. The community sector, on the other hand, with its local knowledge and experience of a place, knows that this is a bridge too far for many people, an objective that is in many places difficult to achieve or, in other places, is simply unachievable. For the key people spearheading the community sector in places, the key to successful regeneration is to be found in different approaches and visions for an alternative social economy that looks beyond quantifiable outputs to qualitative processes that can help transform places in a way that is responsive to the needs and wishes of the people who live there.

Such a truly bottom-up approach is, no doubt unintentionally, being hampered by the structures of public sector funding regimes and formal sector policies. While the community sector is practising initiatives which attempt to engage constructively with individuals and communities trapped in downward spiralling cycles of poverty, the formal sector is failing to recognise and respond to their particular needs. It is, in brief, failing to act locally and, indeed, to acknowledge what this would require in terms of enabling and facilitating public policies and funding regimes.

# 7

# Conclusions and policy implications

## Introduction

This has been a story of social change and the attempts made by people to reconstruct their lives in the context of destructive economic and competitive processes. It has been a story based on experiences contained within the British coalfields. But while the British coalfields have been particularly ravaged by these changes, they are not the only places to suffer. The story told here, then, has a broader provenance. There are perhaps lessons to be learned regarding regeneration strategies in other places (urban and rural) that have been subjected to such changes, most especially when they too were formerly mono-industrial places, dependent on a single economic activity for their economic well-being.

## Issues

The extent to which local initiatives can begin to generate positive change in places such as those that formed the setting and focus of this research will ultimately depend on events and policies elsewhere. It will crucially depend on the extent to which national and supranational policies, funding and tax regimes and institutional systems support rather than impede local communities in generating genuine bottom-up development. This broader macro-economic and policy context is crucial. Locally-based community initiatives cannot substitute for such policies but such policies can be constructed and implemented in ways that help rather than hinder such initiatives. Local initiatives can help create valuable forms of socially-useful work. As such, they can enhance the quality of life of people in deprived places. However, in no

sense should the jobs that they provide be seen as a replacement for well-paid jobs provided in the formal sector of the economy. The issue is how these various forms of work and employment might be best combined to help meet social needs in particular places.

There is a growing recognition that existing top-down formal sector approaches and their related policies and programmes have not led to successful regeneration of the coalfields to date. Their results fall far short of the vision presented by the Coalfields Task Force (1998), which has done much to raise expectations of a better future. Persistent problems and experiences of economic inactivity, poverty and related problems continue to characterise these places. Cuts in local government expenditure have exacerbated the situation, affecting service and facility provision. Such cuts in expenditure have reinforced the isolation of many former coalfield places, making their problems worse. Even when places have a history of successfully attracting FDI, low incomes and the problems of poverty are not necessarily alleviated. Often the prime attraction for such companies is the availability of large numbers of people in search of work. Companies can therefore recruit rigorously and selectively and build up workforces of people willing to work flexibly for low wages, often in non-unionised workplaces. Work is often part-time and sometimes temporary when factories close soon after opening. Furthermore, the work of agencies like British Coal Enterprises has not been as successful as they have claimed in terms of (re)training, employment creation and new business start-ups. There has been little growth of SMEs in the former coalfields and of these very few have been in (high tech) manufacturing. In short, there has been very little success in rebuilding the productive capacity and economies of the former coal districts around new economic activities. As a result they remain blighted by high rates of unemployment, low rates of economic activity, low wages and the environmental and social problems that stem from poverty. Past approaches to regeneration and policies to achieve it have had at best partial and uneven effects in transforming the former coalfields – and in its response to the Coalfields Task Force the New Labour government goes some way to acknowledge this.

It is certainly the case that 'new' government thinking is seeking to target the UK's most deprived places through encouraging partnership working, community empowerment and area-based initiatives that encourage joined-up thinking to tackle the particular needs of local places. These government initiatives have created a context for the regeneration of coalfield places. But it is one that leaves them scarcely better off, with little in the way of new money coming into them. Added to this, the restructuring of EU regional aid has streamlined funding to concentrate greater resources on fewer areas. The criteria currently used in the allocation of funding restrict the eligibility of former coalfield places. While adding little additional financial assistance, the plethora of government policies and programmes often make a confusing and complex context for the regeneration of former coalfield areas. Often it seems that partnerships and community working are less about devolving power to places to regenerate themselves on their own terms and are more about devolving to them the responsibility for their regeneration – but without the commensurate powers and resources. If places fail to pull themselves up by their bootstraps and turn themselves around, then they, in line with current government agendas, have only themselves to blame. There is a strong echo here of earlier generations of policies of 'blaming the victim'.

While policies and programmes recognise the different needs of places, there is still a lack of understanding of the needs of former coalfield areas. Too much emphasis continues to be placed on the need for economic development as the key to unlock the door to regeneration. Often the time horizons are rather short-term

ones. Although the government is keen to espouse the importance of linking social and physical regeneration to economic development for sustainable growth, the emphasis is still on economic development steered by the imperatives of the market. The implications of market domination do not stop there, however. They reverberate down and across agendas, making quantifiable outputs, such as numbers entering into training and formal sector employment, the key goal and measure of success. This particular notion of 'success' is by no means self-evidently the most appropriate one against which to judge community sector initiatives, however. Furthermore, in some of these places 'success' needs to be measured in small steps. In situations in which the simple act of engaging with individuals is difficult, targets defined in terms of success in the formal employment market often seem impossible ones.

There is a wide range of community initiatives, initiated by diverse individuals and organisations (by socially entrepreneurial immigrants, by local residents, or from within formal policy communities) that in various ways are providing alternative forms of work and services in marginalised former coalfield places. Often they are doing so against the odds, in unfavourable circumstances and less than helpful policy and funding environments and in the face of what, to those seeking to animate such initiatives, often seems to be – at best – bureaucratic indifference. Not all succeed in achieving all that they set out to achieve. Some fail. Those that fail tend to be initiated within formal policy communities, and are consequently constrained by formal policy frameworks. Those most likely to succeed are more deeply embedded in their places, with their ear to the ground rather than to the government mouthpiece. Under the circumstances it is perhaps remarkable that so many of them achieve so much, impacting positively on their communities in ways that cannot easily be caught via simple quantifiable indicators of outputs. As a result, there is a tendency to undervalue their contributions to regeneration and to underestimate the public expenditure savings generated by the work of the community sector.

# Policy implications

What then are the implications for regeneration policies in other disadvantaged areas? What lessons might be learned? Some of these are lessons as to what to do, others (equally, if not more, important) are about what not to do.

## Regeneration issues

- 'Regeneration' is by no means a self-evident term. It means different things to different people and organisations with repercussions for aims, objectives and the future vision and role of a place. Formal sector representatives prioritise economic development and the market economy when talking about regeneration. The community sector envisages regeneration to be about the construction of an alternative economy. Partnership is often a necessary condition for accessing public sector funds for regeneration. But different visions of regeneration may cause problems when attempting partnership working. No one view is automatically superior or preferable to another. Whose concept of regeneration is dominant in a particular place, and why? Whose ought to be dominant?

- Regeneration should be seen as a contested, multi-dimensional and multi-faceted process. It must encompass enhancing the quality of the built and natural environments as well as reconstructing the economy. Moreover, there must be a realistic recognition of the limits to the formal sector of the market economy in seeking to regenerate such places. This is not to say that it has no role, but it is to insist that, at best, it will be one part of the solution. However, concerns with issues such as accountability, democratisation, equity and social inclusion should also be central to the regeneration agenda. In some places they may well be the pre-eminent concerns.

## Community issues

- There must be sensitivity to the need for a period of readjustment and grieving as people come to terms with the loss not just of an industry and source of employment but of a culture and way of life. People need time before they are ready to engage in the search for alternative visions of the future for them and for their place. There is, however, no guarantee that their visions of the future will map easily into top-down and externally originating views of regeneration. Whose view does – and should – prevail?

- Community initiatives must, necessarily, play a central role in the regeneration of the poorest and most marginalised places. Such initiatives can play – and have played – a critical role in place-based regeneration. They can, and do, provide alternative sources of work and services that enrich the quality of people's everyday lives and enhance the quality of the environments in which they live.

- Equally, it is important not to be seduced by the concept of 'community'. Often the deployment of the concept of 'community' obfuscates rather than clarifies. Places tend to be socially heterogeneous, with different people having varying, and at times competing, interests. Community development can often mean different things to people in the same place – it too is a contested concept. This reality of 'divided places' needs to be explicitly confronted and dealt with (not swept under some conceptual carpet because it is easier to do so) if place-based regeneration is to be seriously addressed.

- Likewise, and as a corollary, the concept of 'empowerment' requires careful scrutiny if communities really are to be empowered as well as charged with the responsibility of their regeneration. Who is being empowered? By whom? To do what? For and/or to whom? These are not simply academic questions but critical practical questions in the context of devising regeneration strategies in and/or for marginalised and disadvantaged places.

## Funding issues

- Current funding regimes often seem to be more a mechanism for social control than for community empowerment. Seriously addressing place-based regeneration requires, as a necessary (but not sufficient) condition, enabling, facilitating and supportive public sector policies (at EU, national and local government levels). Funding regimes need to be reformed to allow people in their place to define both the content of and delivery mechanisms for regeneration policies.

- There *may* be a need to address issues of capacity building at one or both of two levels. First, to enable the most marginalised individuals to gain the confidence, competencies and skills to enable them to participate as active citizens in local civil societies. Second, to allow new institutions and groups to emerge in disadvantaged places to articulate a collective view as to the content and form of regeneration for their place and as to ways of delivering policies to realise this vision. But there may also be dangers in this emphasis on capacity building. We were struck by the numbers of people involved in community initiatives on the former coalfields who consistently told us that their problem was not lack of capacity – but rather lack of money and resources. They felt confident in their capacity to tackle the problems of their communities but lacked the resources to be able to do so. It is therefore important to be clear as to the precise nature of the problem in a given place – lack of capacity or lack of money? There is a danger that claims as to a lack of local capacity could become a cloak behind which legitimate claims for resources might be hidden.
- In particular, funding regimes need to be radically altered to enable successful good practice to continue to be eligible for public sector funding. Such funding should be available for as long as it is needed. It is facile to pretend that all regeneration problems can ultimately be dealt with by market mechanisms (not least as market mechanisms were often the cause of them in the first place).

### The need to allow an element of risk

- Public sector policies need to be constructed to allow scope for innovation in a variety of ways. As such, they must also allow scope for a degree of risk of failure. Local initiatives that start and then 'fail' may be as important as those that start and then 'succeed', recognising that both success and failure are open to competing interpretations. Perhaps of greatest importance is to encourage a culture that values innovation, not simply in the formal sector of the economy but across a wide range of community and social projects.

### The crucial significance of the specificity of place

- Finally, it is clear that coalfield communities share many serious problems. There certainly needs to be a framework of policies and resources at national and EU level that recognises the extent and severity of these shared problems. At the same time, there needs to be sufficient flexibility to allow policy responses to be customised to address the specific problems of particular places and reflect the aspirations and objectives of the people who live there. It is therefore important to stress there are no ready-made 'off-the-shelf' solutions that can be taken from one place and mechanistically implanted in another to effect its successful regeneration. On the other hand, there are lessons that can be learned, principles of good practice that can be identified, as long as these are then modified and tailored to the specific context of another place. A regeneration strategy based on slavish imitation is doomed to failure. On the other hand, learning is both possible and desirable, provided that it respects the specific needs of people in their places.

# References

Adamson, D. and Jones, S. (1996) *The South Wales Valleys: Continuity and change*, Pontypridd: Regional Research Programme, University of Glamorgan.

Ahmad, Y. and Miller, C. (1997) 'Community development at the crossroads: a way forward', *Policy & Politics*, vol 25, no 3, pp 269-84.

Beatty, C., Fothergill, S., Gore, T. and Herrington, A. (1997) *The real level of unemployment*, Sheffield: Centre for Regional Economic and Social Research, Sheffield Hallam University.

BCE (British Coal Enterprises) (1996) *A review of activities: Helping create jobs*, London: BCE.

BCRS (Bryncynon Community Revival Strategy Ltd) (1998) *Business plan into the millennium 1998-2003*, Bryncynon: BCRS.

BCRS (1999) *As one: A book of words and pictures by and about people of the Cynon Valley in South Wales*, Penywaun: Penywaun Publications.

CTF (Coalfields Task Force) (1998) *Making the difference: A new start for England's coalfield communities*, London: DETR.

DETR (Department of the Environment, Transport and the Regions) (1997) *Building partnerships for prosperity: Sustainable growth, competitiveness and employment in the English regions*, London: The Stationery Office.

DETR (1998) *Making the difference: A new start for England's coalfield communities: The government's response to the Coalfields Task Force Report*, London: DETR.

East Durham Task Force (1997) *East Durham Programme for Action: The road to success 1997-2001*, Durham: Durham County Council.

East Midlands Objective 2 Area (1997) *Single Programming Document 1: January 1997-31 December 1999*, Unpublished document.

Fernhill Estate Young Women (1999) *a bad name? a book of voices*, Penywaun: Penywaun Publications.

Fothergill, S. and Guy, N. (1994) *An evaluation of British Coal Enterprises*, Coalfield Communities Campaign.

Hudson, R. (1995) 'The role of foreign inward investment', in L. Evans, P. Johnson and B. Thomas (eds) *The northern region economy: Progress and prospects in the North of England*, London: Mansell.

Hudson, R. and Williams, A.M. (1995) *Divided Britain*, 2nd edn, Chichester: Wiley.

Local Government International Bureau (1999) *European Information Service*, issue 201, 26 July.

Lovering, J. (1996) 'New myths of the Welsh economy', *Planet*, no 116, pp 6-16.

Mansfield District Council (1998) *Marketing Mansfield Initiative: Business Guide*, Mansfield: MDC.

NOMIS (National Online Manpower Information System) http://www.durham.ac.uk/ ~dnm0www/

North Nottinghamshire Director of Public Health (1997) *Annual Report: Health into 2000 and beyond.*

ONS (Office for National Statistics) (1997) *New Earnings Survey,* London: The Stationery Office.

ONS (1998) *Regional Trends 33,* London: The Stationery Office.

Pearce, J. (1993) *At the heart of the community economy: Community enterprise in a changing world,* London: Calouste Gulbenkian Foundation.

RCTCBC (Rhondda Cynon Taff County Borough Council) (1998) *Rhondda Cynon Taff: A vision for business success,* Abercynon: Economic Development Unit, RCTCBC.

Redwood, F. (1999) 'Bargains await you away from the scrum', *The Times,* 6 October.

Rees, G. and Thomas, M. (1991) 'Enterprise and coal miners', Paper delivered to British Sociological Association Conference, Plymouth, 4-6 September.

Social Exclusion Unit (1998) *Bringing Britain together: A national strategy for neighbourhood renewal,* London: The Stationery Office.

South Wales Coalfield RECHAR 2 Programme 1994-1997.

VIAE (1999) *Draft Business Plan 1999-2001,* Unpublished document.

Welsh Office (1998) *Pathway to prosperity: A new economic agenda for Wales,* Cardiff: Welsh Office.

# Appendix A: Community initiatives studied in the research project

Arts Factory
Bilsthorpe Youth Club
Blaenllechau Community Regeneration
Boughton Pumping Station
Bryncynon Community Revival Strategy
Phil Cope (Valley and Vale/Write for Cynon)
Cynon Valley Credit Union
Dulais Valley Partnership
Girls' Project (Boughton and Ollerton)
Group preparing to set up Steering Committee for Mansfield Credit Union
Group preparing to set up Steering Committee for Ollerton Credit Union
Mansfield Community Development Project
Mansfield Counselling Service
Mansfield LETS Initiative (Mansfield Unemployed Workers Centre)
Mansfield Woodhouse Community Development Group
Mansfield Woodhouse IT Cybercafé
New Dawn Arts Project (Mansfield)
Ollerton and Boughton Community Development Project
Ollerton and Boughton Women's Centre
Ollerton and District Economic Forum
Penrhiwceiber Community Revival Strategy Group
Penrhys Partnership
Penygraig Community Project (Valley Kids from April 1999)
Penyrenglyn Project
Penywaun Enterprise Partnership
Perthcelyn Residents' and Tenants' Association
Rhondda Cynon Taff Community Arts
Rhondda Cynon Taff Credit Union Forum
Shirebrook Development Trust
The Furniture Project (Boughton)
Tichfield Ward (Mansfield Diamond Partnership – SRB Project)
Tonyrefail Credit Union
Tower Colliery
Valleys Childcare Ltd
Valleys Furniture Recycling
Valleys Initiative for Adult Education
Virtual Village: Connecting the Coalfield (RCC – Nottinghamshire)
Warsop Vale Residents' Association

# Appendix B: Formal sector organisations and agencies

Representatives of these organisations were interviewed as part of the study.

Aberdare College
Business Link (St Helens)
Citizens Advice Bureau (Ollerton and District)
Coal Industry Social Welfare Organisation (North East)
Coal Industry Social Welfare Organisation (North West)
Coal Industry Social Welfare Organisation (Mansfield)
County Durham and Darlington Training and Enterprise Council
Dukeries Community College
Durham Cooperative Association
Durham Constabulary
Durham County Council (Social Services)
Durham County Council (Economic Development)
Durham County Council (Education and Careers)
Durham Health Authority
Easington District Council (Economic Development and Tourism)
Easington District Council (Housing)
East Durham Community College
East Durham Community Development Initiative
East Durham Development Agency
English Partnerships (North East)
English Partnerships (East Midlands)
English Partnerships (North West)
Government Office for North East
Government Office for North West
Government Office for East Midlands
Groundwork (Mansfield and Ashfield)
Groundwork (East Durham)
Mansfield 2010
Mansfield Diamond Partnership
Mansfield District Council (Economic Development)
Mansfield District Council (Housing)
Mansfield District Council (Community Economic Development)
Mansfield Training Initiative
Mansfield Unemployed Workers Centre
MEP: Ken Coates
MEP: Wayne David
MEP: Stephen Hughes
MP: Ann Clywd (Cynon Valley)
MP: John Cummings (Easington)

MP: Alan Meale (Mansfield)

Merseyside Police Authority

Merseyside Training and Enterprise Council

Mid Glamorgan Training and Enterprise Council

National Union of Miners (Durham)

North Nottinghamshire College

North Nottinghamshire Health Authority

North Nottinghamshire Training and Enterprise Council

Nottinghamshire Cooperative

Nottinghamshire Constabulary (Mansfield/Ashfield Division)

Nottinghamshire County Council (Economic and Planning)

Peterlee GP

Rhondda Cynon Taff County Borough Council (Social Services)

Rhondda Cynon Taff County Borough Council (Policy Research and European Affairs Unit/ Economic Development)

Rhondda Cynon Taff County Borough Council (Housing)

Rural Community Council (Nottinghamshire – Rural Action/Delegated Fund)

South Wales Health Authority

South Wales Police

St Helens Chamber of Commerce, Training and Enterprise

St Helens and Knowsley Health Authority

St Helens Metropolitan Borough Council (Economic Development)

St Helens Metropolitan Borough Council (Housing)

St Helens Metropolitan Borough Council (Education and Careers)

Sunderland Unemployment Centre

Voluntary Care for the Unemployed (Aberdare)

Wales Cooperative Centre

Welsh Development Agency

Welsh Office

# Also available from The Policy Press:

## Neighbourhood regeneration

*Resourcing community involvement*

Pete Duncan and Sally Thomas
Social regeneration consultants

*Neighbourhood regeneration* looks at community capacity building within area regeneration programmes in urban areas in the UK and examines pertinent issues and current resources and practice. The authors frame this review within the context of the government's national strategy for neighbourhood renewal, *Bringing Britain together*, and the Local Government Association's New Commitment to Regeneration initiative.

The report aims to establish:

- what works and what does not;

- how existing funding might be improved;

- what additional resources might be needed to fill the gaps in current provision;

- who should provide these additional resources;

- how resources might best be targeted;

- how resourcing community involvement can be linked to emerging proposals for neighbourhood management and joined-up action by regeneration agencies.

Contents: Introduction; The policy context; The importance of community capacity building; Delivering a community-based approach to neighbourhood regeneration; An overview of current practice; A strategic approach to filling the gaps; Resourcing the funding gaps; Conclusion: a Neighbourhood Empowerment fund.

Paperback £12.95 (US$23.50) • ISBN 1 86134 227 6

297 x 210mm • 52 pages • March 2000

Area Regeneration Series in association with the Joseph Rowntree Foundation